THE
USS SAGINAW
IN ALASKA WATERS
1868-1869

Alaska History No. 46

THE USS SAGINAW IN ALASKA WATERS 1867-1868

by
ROBERT N. DeARMOND

Edited
by
RICHARD A. PIERCE

THE LIMESTONE PRESS
Kingston, Ontario : Fairbanks, Alaska
1997

Box 1604
Kingston, Ontario K7L 3N6
Canada

U.S. Office:
The Limestone Press
℅ History Department
University of Alaska Fairbanks
Fairbanks, Alaska 99775-0860
U.S.A.

Distributed by University of Alaska Press.
P. O. Box 756240
Fairbanks, Alaska 99775-6240

International Standard Book Number 1-895901-10-3

Production: J. Ketz

TO DALE BURLISON DEARMOND, who has supported my endeavors and put up with my idiosyncracies during sixty years of married life, this volume is affectionately dedicated.

U.S. Steamer *Saginaw* – Fourth Rate
Built at the Navy Yard, Mare Island, California, in 1859.

CONTENTS

ILLUSTRATIONS

MAPS

FOREWORD

Part of the pleasure of historical research comes from seeking and sometimes finding previously unknown material which can clarify the past. Thus in 1990 I wrote Marla Daily, President of the Santa Cruz Island Foundation of Santa Barbara, with a query about early Russian fur hunters in California's Channel Islands. In reply she mentioned that during her own research she had come upon a diary by Peveril Meigs, kept during a trip to Alaska in 1868. The diary had sat for decades in a trunk in Meigs' granddaughter-in-law's home in Carpentaria, California. It was an account of a voyage in 1868 on the U.S. Navy vessel *Saginaw*, which took punitive measures against several Tlingit settlements in Southeast Alaska.

While looking for more information about the *Saginaw*'s voyage, I found that the well-known Alaska historian Robert DeArmond had been working for several years on that very subject. It appeared logical to combine our two enterprises, hence the present book.

Loren M. Meigs, a grandson of Peveril Meigs, kindly gave permission to publish the journal and provided information concerning his grandfather. Peveril Meigs was born February 27, 1847. When he was 21 he went out west to California. Family tradition has it that his father wanted to get him away from a female friend (whom, however, he later married). While in San Francisco, Meigs met his cousin, Lieutenant-Commander Richard Worsam Meade. Both were nephews of General George Gordon Meade, of Civil War fame. Lieutenant-Commander Meade, now 31, noted for his bluntness and strict execution of duty, had served with distinction in the Civil War, and in 1863 had helped to put down the New

York City draft riots. Now taking command of the *Saginaw*, about to sail to Alaska, he invited his young cousin to come along.

For Peveril Meigs the voyage in rain-soaked southeastern Alaska was only a pleasant interlude. He worked in New York until 1887, when he bought a 104-acre ranch on La Mesa, in Santa Barbara. As a retired gentleman farmer, he engaged in making and bottling highly priced olive oil from his olive orchard, and dry bean farming. His descendants have included a son, Peveril Meigs, Jr. (1874-1926), whose Santa Cruz Island journal was published by the Santa Cruz Island Foundation in 1990, and grandsons Peveril Meigs III (b. 1903), author of a book on Baja California, and Loren Meigs. The latter kindly gave the family's approval of publication of the diary and furnished a photograph of his grandfather. None could be found of Lieutenant-Commander Mitchell, but the Civil War Library and Museum, of Philadelphia, found a wartime photo of Lieutenant-Commander Richard Worsam Meade. The journal *Alaska History*, Anchorage, has given permission to publish the photo of Saginaw Jake, which appeared with an article by Robert DeArmond: "Saginaw Jake: Navy Hostage, Indian Policeman, Celebrity (*Alaska Journal*, Spring 1990, vol. 5, no. 1, pp. 23-33).

The Appendix contains two letters from Lieutenant-Commander John G. Mitchell, and two articles about Alaska by Lieutenant-Commander Meade (one somewhat abridged), which were published in *Appleton's Journal*, New York, in 1871. The Chinook Jargon word list was probably compiled by Lieutenant-Commander Mitchell (see letter of August 31, 1868), but was among Peveril Meigs' papers and doubtless aided communication with the "pretty young klootchmen" he met during the voyage.

The photographs of Sitka, Fort Wrangel and Fort Tongass, taken in July and August, 1868, depict the two U.S. Military posts, just established, and some local residents. They were taken by Eadweard Muybridge, the well-known San Francisco photographer, who accompanied

FOREWORD

General Henry W. Halleck, commander of the Military Division of the Pacific, on a tour of Alaska on the steamer *Pacific*. Aside from several photographs taken in 1865 by a member of the Western Union Telegraph Expedition, those by Muybridge would seem to be the first ever taken in Alaska.

The *Saginaw*'s course through the many islands and channels of the Archipelago can be traced on the map reprinted here from Alexander Badlam's *The Wonders of Alaska*, published by the Bancroft Company, San Francisco, in 1890.

Spelling varied. Hence the present-day Wrangell was earlier Wrangel or Wrangle. Also Tchillkat (now Chilkat) and Tungass (Tongass), etc.

The structural drawing mentioned in the description of the *Saginaw* could not be found.

— R. A. Pierce, Editor

PREFACE

THE SHIP

The USS *Saginaw*, which made two cruises to Southeastern Alaska in the years 1868 and 1869, was known for a number of "firsts." She was the first United States warship built on the Pacific Coast and the first to be built at the Mare Island Navy Yard at Vallejo, California. And although at least four U.S. Navy vessels had traveled to Alaska since 1867 when Russia transferred the territory to the United States, the *Saginaw* was the first to travel the inner waterways of Southeastern Alaska. She traversed Wrangell Narrows several times and was undoubtedly the first American steamer to do so.

In an Act approved June 12, 1858, Congress appropriated funds for the Navy Department to build twelve propeller driven sloops and one side paddle steamer. The latter was to be a dispatch boat for the Asiatic Squadron, stationed off the coast of China. It was decided to build the steamer on the Pacific Coast, and that meant building it at the Mare Island Navy Yard, the only such facility on the West Coast at that time.

Specifications for the steamer were set forth in a letter from the Navy's Bureau of Construction in Washington to the Commandant at the Mare Island Navy Yard.[1]

The vessel was to have a length of 155 feet, an extreme breadth of 26 feet and its greatest draft was not to exceed 8 feet. It would be very lightly rigged, the steam machinery, including water in the boilers, was estimated to weigh 80 tons and displacement was estimated to be 508 tons. It was proposed that the ship, while on station, should have 90 days provisions and 18 days water for 50 persons and would stow 100 tons of coal.

The specifications called for an armament of "a 32-pd gun on a pivot and two boat guns." A later description of the vessel, however, listed her guns as one 50-pounder Dahlgren rifle, one 32-pounder and two 24-pounder rifles.[2]

The vessel's keel, stem, stempost and knightheads were to be of live oak and her frames of white oak. The garboard strakes were to be of white oak 5 inches thick; the next planks 4 inches thick and the remaining planks 3 inches thick. Planking on the main deck was to be of yellow pine and berth deck planking of white pine.

Despite these specifications, two sources state that she was built of laurel.[3] That seems an unlikely material for shipbuilding, although perhaps laurel oak, also known as shingle oak, was intended.

The Sail Plan

The vessel's sail plan is not mentioned in the specifications from the Bureau of Construction, but there is a list of her masts and spars and from that it is evident that she was to be rigged as a half brig, known to sailors as an hermaphrodite brig, with square sails on the foremast and fore-and-aft sails on the mainmast.

The foremast was to be 65 feet with a diameter of 18 inches, with a fore topmast of 27 feet and 8½ inches diameter; fore topgallant mast of 12 feet 6 inches and 6 inch diameter, and the whole to be topped by a pole 6 feet high, no diameter given. On this mast were the foreyard, 44 feet 6 inches long and with a diameter of 8¼ inches; fore topsail yard 30 feet long and 6 inches in diameter, and a fore topgallant yard 19 feet 6 inches long and 4 1/8 inches in diameter.

The mainmast towered 68 feet with a diameter of 17 inches. Then there was a topmast 28 feet high and 8 inches in diameter, a topgallant mast 13 feet high with a diameter of 5½ inches. The mainmast pole was 7 feet high. The main boom was 56 feet long, 10 2/4 inches diameter, and the gaff 26 feet 7 inches long and 7 inches in diameter.

The bowsprit extended 15 feet outboard with a diameter of 16¼ inches, and beyond that was 17 feet of jibboom, 8¼ inches in diameter.

The *Saginaw* apparently had at least three different sail plans during her career. There was the half-brig plan with which she started out and which is shown in the drawing. The only photograph that has been found of her shows her as a full-rigged brig, with yards on both masts. And Donald L. Canney in his book *The Old Steam Navy* says that she was rigged as a topsail schooner.[4]

What rig the *Saginaw* carried in Alaska waters has not been determined. Entries in the ship's log mention setting the foresail and the topsails, but a foresail may either be hung from a yard or lashed to a boom. It is probable that she was a topsail schooner.

THE POWER PLANT

According to Donald L. Canney in his book *The Old Steam Navy*, the *Saginaw*'s engines were unique among American warships and the type had been used previously in only one Navy vessel, some eight years earlier.

There were two inclined oscillating engines each with a cylinder 39½ inches in diameter and with a piston having a four-foot stroke. Each cylinder was equipped with trunnions and they were mounted side by side, aligned fore and aft with the trunnions supported on stout A-frames. The piston rods were directly connected to the cranks of the shaft on which the paddle wheels — the Navy called them water wheels — were mounted. These wheels were of wrought iron, 20 feet in diameter and with paddles six feet in length. In the housing of each wheel there was to be a surface condenser capable of supplying 150 gallons of water a day.

The engines were designed to operate under 30 pounds of steam pressure and to turn the wheels at a maximum of 26 revolutions a minute. The cylinders worked opposite each other, one moving up 40 degrees while the other moved down the same amount, and the piston rods could be disconnected from the crank shaft when the vessel was under sail alone or, if need be, so the ship could operate on one engine.

To furnish steam to the engines there were two boilers, oval in shape and each with three furnaces. Each boiler had 600 brass tubes, placed vertically. And in each of the six furnaces there was 15 square feet of grate bars, specified to be of "the best quality of charcoal iron." The boilers were covered with an inch and a half of felt which was sewed to No. 1 canvas which in turn was covered by tongue-and-grove lumber held in place by iron straps.

The engines and boilers were built in San Francisco by Peter Donahue's Union Iron Works, under the inspection of George Sewall, Chief Engineer, U.S. Navy. One newspaper described the engines as "the first marine engines constructed upon the Pacific Coast," but this was not exactly true.[5] Some twenty years earlier an engineer named Edward Moore and employed by the Russian-American Company, had built the engines for two launches, one of which had been taken to California and had run on the Sacramento River. Beyond doubt, however, the *Saginaw*'s engines were the first built on the coast under the American flag.

The Bureau of Construction had estimated that the engines for the *Saginaw* would cost, on the Atlantic Coast about $36,000 with about $6,000 additional for the surface condensers. There was no mention of the boilers in this estimate. The cost of the power plant, including the boilers and condensers, was just under $80,000 at San Francisco.[6]

The Launching

The ship was launched at the Mare Island Navy Yard on March 3, 1859. No name had been assigned to her and she was christened by the daughter of the commandant, Captain R. B. Cunningham, with the name *Toucey* in honor of Secretary of the Navy Isaac Toucey. But Secretary Toucey would have none of that and when the ship was commissioned, on January 5, 1860, it was with the name *Saginaw* for the Saginaw River of Michigan which flows into Saginaw Bay of Lake Huron.

Early Career

Two months after she was placed in commission the *Saginaw* sailed from San Francisco on March 8, 1860, and reached Shanghai, China, on May 12. She then served with the East India Squadron, mostly cruising along the Chinese coast to protect American citizens and suppress pirates, but also made one trip to Japan. On June 30, 1861, while she was searching for a missing boat from an American bark, the *Saginaw* was fired upon by a battery at the entrance to Quinhon Bay, Cochin, China. She returned the fire and silenced the battery. This may have been the only time in her career when the *Saginaw* was fired upon or returned the fire of an aggressor.

At Whampoa in January 1862 the ship was found to be quite rotten.[7] She was decommissioned and sent home in July.

It was not until December that the ship was relaunched and she was not recommissioned until March 23, 1863. By then the carnage of the Civil War was at full gallop and the *Saginaw* joined the Pacific Squadron which was patrolling the coast to prevent Confederate activity. The *Saginaw* went first to Puget Sound then south to Mexico and Central America to protect Union interests there. She also escorted vessels of the Pacific Mail Steamship Company which carried bullion from the gold fields of California. For a short time in 1865 the vessel was assigned to the Revenue Marine Service.

After the war ended the *Saginaw* again went to Puget Sound in August 1866 to support the increasing number of settlers in that area. While on that duty she assisted the Western Union Telegraph in laying a cable to bring telegraphic service to the region. She returned to Mare Island in December 1866.

The ship's next assignment was again on the coast of Mexico where she was cruising at the beginning of the year 1868 just prior to her first voyage to Alaska. For her post-Alaska career and last voyage, see Chapter 11.

NOTES

1. Dated July 17, 1858, signed by John Senthall, Chief of the Bureau, and addressed to Captain R. B. Cunningham.

2. Donald L. Canney, *The Old Steam Navy*, 2 vols. (Annapolis, Maryland: Naval Institute Press, 1990), vol. 1, p. 88; and James L. Mooney and Richard T. Speer, eds., *Dictionary of American Fighting Ships*, 8 vols. (Washington: Navy Dept., Office of the Chief of Naval Operations, Naval History Division, 1959-1981), v. 7, p. 230.

3. Donald L. Canney, *op. cit.*, vol 1., p. 88; and *Alta California, op. cit.*

4. Donald L. Canney, *op. cit.*, vol. 1, p. 88.

5. The *Herald* (San Francisco), September 14, 1859.

6. *Ibid.*

7. Donald L. Canney, *op. cit.*, vol. 1, p. 88. The fact that she developed rot so early lends some credence to the report that she was built, at least partly, of laurel wood rather than oak.

ACKNOWLEDGEMENTS

Many individuals have given assistance in rounding up the material for this account of the Alaska voyages of the USS *Saginaw*, and especially the following:

Dr. Richard A. Pierce, University of Alaska Fairbanks, who discovered the manuscript of the Meigs diary as well as several other documents relating to the voyage.

The Alaska State Library at Juneau and especially Jeff Rothal in Interlibrary Loans and Kay Shelton, India Spartz and Gladi Kulp in Historical Collections.

The Kettleson Memorial Library in Sitka, especially Nancy Gustavson, Director; and Kathy Parker, Interlibrary Loan librarian, and Patsy Young.

Austen Hemion, maritime historian, Seattle.

David R. Chamberlin, Victoria, B.C., who provided items from Victoria newspapers.

William Kooiman, Librarian at the San Francisco Maritime National Historical Park, Fort Mason, San Francisco, Calif.

Sue Lemmon, Historian, Mare Island Naval Station at Vallejo, California.

Last but by no means least, my wife, Dale, whose skill as a proof-reader far exceeds my own.

I

FROM CALIFORNIA TO ALASKA

During the first three months of the year 1868 the USS *Saginaw*, in charge of Lieut.-Commander John G. Mitchell, USN, was cruising off the coast of Mexico and in the Gulf of California with occasional calls at Guaymas, La Paz, Mazatlan and San Blas.[1] Toward the end of March she headed for San Francisco where she arrived on April 7. She did not go up to Mare Island but anchored off San Francisco while outfitting for her Alaska voyage.

The *Saginaw* put to sea at 10:30 P.M., on April 18, 1868, bound for Alaska. She made the voyage, according to the annual report of the Secretary of the Navy, "for the purpose of making explorations and surveys and of determining the most suitable harbors and anchorages on the coast and in the adjacent islands."[2] She would, it turned out, do a good deal more than that during the voyage.

The ship's officers were:

Lieut.-Commander John G. Mitchell, commanding
Acting Master and executive officer C. C. Bunker
Acting Master J. B. Wood
Ensigns A. H. Vail and J. K. P. Ragsdale
First Assistant Engineer Thomas McCausland
Acting Third Assistant Engineers A. L. Grow, E. T. Peake, W. J. Faul and H. Litchfield
Assistant Surgeon W. H. Whidon
Assistant Paymaster C. H. Lockwood
Mates William Kneeland, Philip Randall and John Ponte
Captain's Clerk C. L. Hidden

It appears that at least one of the mates may have been a civilian employee rather than regular Navy officer. Kneeland resigned and left the ship in mid-voyage.

There were 48 enlisted men in the crew according to the muster roll prepared when the ship was at Hamilton Bay, Alaska, on June 30. The ship may have been short-handed, in quality if not in numbers. They were reported as 13 petty officers, 6 seamen, 9 ordinary seamen, 8 landsmen, 2 boys, 5 firemen and 6 coal heavers.

It was a period when the Navy was having difficulty recruiting bluejackets and several of the *Saginaw*'s men were signed up in San Francisco only hours before she sailed. Many of the enlistments were for one year only; others were for two and three years.

Just over half of the enlisted men were foreign born. The British Isles was the birthplace of many but others came from Prussia, the Philippines, Panama, Norway and Mexico. The Americans, including one Indian, hailed from places across the country from Maine to California. The "Occupation" column of the muster roll shows 17 mariners, a student, 2 caulkers, 2 cooks, a barber, a shoemaker, a butcher, a brass finisher, 2 coal heavers, a mason, a hunter, several laborers and several listed as having no occupation.

Whatever their origins or occupations, the crew was composed of small men. Only 13 of the 48 were taller than 5 feet 6 inches. The tallest man stood 5 feet 9 inches. There were many recorded on the muster roll at 5 feet 2, 5-3, and 5-4. A check of the muster rolls of other ships at that period shows the same pattern and it can only be concluded that the average man in America in 1868 was much shorter than the average man today.

It was a pretty mixed bag that answered the roll call aboard the *Saginaw*. The Navy was taking what it could get, and what it got for the Alaska voyage was a lot of disciplinary problems. The most frequent infractions were insolence toward an officer, disregard of orders, overstaying leave and returning aboard drunk. Punishment was commonly confinement in single or double irons — handcuffs or handcuffs and leg irons — for from one to several days on a diet of bread and water. If the confinement was a long one the prisoner received full rations every seventh day. There were several desertions during the voyage.

The *Saginaw* had an easy run up the coasts of California, Oregon and Washington. Steam was used all the way, with some of the fore-and-aft sails set a part of the time. The square foretopsail was unfurled only once and then for just a few hours.

At 8 P.M. on April 23 the anchor was dropped in the harbor at the British naval base of Esquimault on Vancouver Island, just west of Victoria. This was a new naval yard, fully established only four years earlier, but it was able to fill the American warship's needs. The ship took aboard 60 tons of coal, 45 pounds each of beef and vegetables and an unspecified quantity and variety of "wardroom stores."

The weather was fine and on two days the crew was engaged in painting the ship and also was drilled with single sticks. On Sunday, April 26, several of the crew had liberty. Then on the 29th at 3:40 P.M. — the Navy had not yet adopted the 24-hour clock — the anchor was raised, they stood out of the harbor and picked up Pilot Robert Hicks.

Hicks signed on as pilot for the voyage at $150 a month. He also served as interpreter for at least some of the Indian languages. He was 40 years old, born in England and had served in both the British and American Navies. He had also made a voyage aboard a whaler, then operated his own schooner on Puget Sound before he signed on as an officer aboard vessels of the Hudson's Bay Company. At that time the mainland portion of Southeastern Alaska was under lease to the British company and its vessels made trading voyages to Alaska waters. Hicks was probably one of the most knowledgeable pilots for the channels of British Columbia and Southeast Alaska. On this voyage he piloted the *Saginaw* through Wrangell Narrows several times and she was undoubtedly the first American steamer and certainly the first American Navy vessel to traverse that waterway.

A point of Mitkof Island in the narrows is named for him. When he retired from piloting he became master of the Fraser River lightship until 1900 when he moved to Victoria, B.C., where he died in 1908 at the age of 81.

Hicks evidently knew the channels well, for the *Saginaw*, in that time of few aids to navigation, ran at night. It was necessary to anchor occasionally because of fog and she also anchored in Safety Cove, just north of Queen Charlotte Sound, for boiler repairs. Brief stops were also made at Bella Bella and Fort Simpson and she crossed the boundary at 54°40′ into Alaska waters at about 9:15 o'clock on Sunday morning, May 3. The fact was not noted in the deck log. At 10:15, however, it was noted that the ship was abreast Cape Fox.

That afternoon Ensign Vail wrote in the log that the ship was steaming up Tongass Narrows. Where did he get that name? It could only have come from Pilot Hicks and indicates that the name had been in use on Hudson's Bay Company vessels although the *Dictionary of Alaska Place Names* states that the narrows were named in the 1878-1880 period.

At 6:10 A.M. on May 4 the ship entered Wrangell Narrows with bare steerage way and leads going on both bows. At 7:10 A.M. the ship went aground. Soundings were taken, showing 11 feet of water on the starboard side, 10 feet to port, 11 feet forward and 10 aft. It must have been a rising tide because at 7:15 the ship was afloat. They passed on through the narrows and into Prince Frederick Sound without further difficulty and at 6:15 P.M. dropped anchor just inside the entrance to "Cake Bay." Today it is known as Saginaw Bay. That evening Ensign Ragsdale was sent to sound the harbor.

The ship got under way at 4:20 A.M. and at 6:30 anchored off the Indian village of "Kyke" at the head of the bay. Commander Mitchell and Ensigns Vail and Ragsdale, in three boats, spent all that day and the next surveying the harbor. It seems probable that Commander Mitchell had been instructed to find a place suitable for a Navy depot and likely that Pilot Hicks had suggested "Cake" Bay, which on June 25 Mitchell would name

Saginaw Bay. Surveys were made in other bays during the voyage, but none was as thorough as the one of Saginaw Bay.

On May 7 the *Saginaw* got under weigh at 3:55 A.M. for Sitka where she arrived at 3:30 P.M. and "made our numbers" to the USS *Jamestown* which was moored in the channel between Japonski Island and the Indian village. The *Saginaw* dropped her anchor close by and borrowed a 600-pound kedge from the *Jamestown* for a stern anchor. Captain King of the *Jamestown* went aboard the *Saginaw* for a courtesy visit.

The *Jamestown*, built in 1844, had the sails and rigging of a full-rigged ship, had no steam power and was classed by the Navy as a sloop-of-war. She was fast under sail and had proved it in 1847 when she carried 800 tons of relief supplies to famine-stricken Ireland. She crossed from Boston to Queenstown in 15 days 3 hours, anchor to anchor. This turn of speed served her well during her early tours of duty which were in the South Pacific chasing slavers bound for Africa or the Caribbean. She out-sailed and captured several of them.

During the early part of the Civil War the *Jamestown* joined the Atlantic Blockading Squadron, but in 1862 she was sent to the Pacific to protect American commerce. She searched for but did not find the Confederate raider *Shenandoah* when that vessel was preying on the Yankee whaling fleet in the western Pacific and Bering Sea. The *Jamestown* would remain in Pacific waters until 1882 when she went back to the Atlantic.

The *Jamestown* and the USS *Resaca* had been stationed at Panama the previous summer and some members of their crews had contracted yellow fever. The ships were sent north to Sitka in the territory newly acquired from Russia to expose them to the salubrious effects of the colder climate. The *Jamestown* had arrived at Sitka on September 11 and the *Resaca* two days later. Both had been present for the change of flags on October 18, 1867. The *Resaca* had gone south in January 1868; the *Jamestown* would remain at Sitka as a store-ship and guard-ship until May 30. She would return in June 1879 for a two-year stay.

The month of May is often a pleasant one at Sitka, but 1868 was not one of those years, at least during the 17 days the *Saginaw* was at anchor in the harbor. The log recorded two gales, temperatures mostly in the 40s, rain, drizzle and two days with thick fog and one with hail. Only on May 24th, just before they left Sitka, did it clear up and the temperature reach 60 degrees.

While in port they coaled the ship, taking 69 tons from a lighter. The crew also cut wood, in the rain, for the galley range, and hauled water in one of the boats from what became known as Jamestown Bay. On a small stream in the eastern corner of the bay a small dam had been built and a flume installed to carry water out past the high water mark. At high tide a ship's boat could be positioned under the end of the flume and filled with water, then towed to the ship. One of the *Saginaw*'s boats held 200 gallons of water and made five trips to the flume. On one trip for water a crew member went AWOL and there is nothing in the log to indicate that he ever returned on board.

On Sunday, May 17, there was a log book entry: "Sent an officer on shore to receive the ship's apothecary from the authorities, having been confined in the calaboose." Whether the "authorities" were the Army or consent government of Sitka is not stated, but the calaboose was undoubtedly the guard house in the log barracks built by the Russians and used by both the military and civil authorities.

On May 19, according to the log: "Received from the store-ship *Jamestown* 45 pea jackets, 20 blankets, 5 mattresses, 50 over shirts, 50 Satine A pants, 50 blue cloth trowsers, 50 caps." Two days later a quantity of "rigging gear, rope, etc.," were received from the store-ship as well as ten men. They were on loan, perhaps to work on the *Saginaw*'s rigging, and returned to their own ship two days later.

The Cutter *Wayanda* of the U.S. Revenue Marine Service arrived at Sitka on May 23, and on the following day the *Saginaw* received 50 boiler tubes from her. At some time during her Sitka stay the *Saginaw* loaded Army quartermaster stores to take to what was recorded as "Stachine" and is now Wrangell, where the Army was building a fort.

The *Saginaw* left Sitka at 7 o'clock A.M. on May 25, stopped at "Cake Harbor" and "received on board the chief of the Indians as a passenger." It is unclear whether the chief went to "Stachine" or whether he remained aboard, perhaps as a guide or interpreter, while Commander Mitchell inquired into the wreck of the schooner *Growler*, about which he had no doubt heard in Sitka.

That evening the *Saginaw* anchored in "Clear Cove, Bunker Bay." Today it is known as Portage Bay. Commander Mitchell obviously intended to name it for his executive officer, Master C. C. Bunker, and it is unfortunate the name didn't stick. Alaska has a surplus of places named Portage Bay. As for the cove just inside the entrance to the bay, where the *Saginaw* apparently anchored, it bears no name on today's charts.

At 1:15 A.M. on May 27 the *Saginaw* "anchored off Stachine Village and began discharging Quartermaster stores for the Army." On this harbor in 1834 the Russian-American Company had built Redoubt St. Dionisius in an effort to prevent the Hudson's Bay Company from entering the Stikine River. This was contrary to a treaty previously signed by Russia and Great Britain and the upshot was that Russia turned the site over to the Hudson's Bay Company and leased the mainland of Southeastern Alaska to it as well. The British fur company called its post Fort Stikine and maintained it until 1849, then abandoned it. Since then and until the summer of 1868, except for a brief flurry in 1861 when small quantities of gold were found on the upper Stikine River, the place had been just another Tlingit Indian village.

When the *Saginaw* arrived in the bay on May 27, Captain J. H. Smith and a contingent of enlisted men from Company E, 2nd U.S. Artillery, were busy building what would become Fort Wrangell. The *Saginaw* remained at anchor for four days and left at 5:10 P.M. on May 30 and headed south toward Cape Chacon to try to learn the fate of the people who had been aboard the schooner *Growler*.

NOTES

1. According to the entries in her deck log for that period. *See* U.S. Department of the Navy, Records of the Bureau of Naval Personnel, Record Group 24, M/F 145, Roll 2, Log of the USS *Saginaw*, 1/1/1868 - 4/17/1869; Archives, Alaska and Polar Regions Department, Elmer E. Rasmuson Library, University of Alaska Fairbanks. The entry on the *Saginaw* in the *Dictionary of American Naval Fighting Ships*, published by the Navy, seems to indicate that she was at the Mare Island through 1867 and until she sailed for Alaska. *See* James L. Mooney and Richard T. Speer, eds., *Dictionary of American Fighting Ships*, 8 vols. (Washington: Navy Dept., Office of the Chief of Naval Operations, Naval History Division, 1959-1981), v. 7, p. 230.

2. "Report of the Secretary of the Navy," December 7, 1868, page XV.

II

THE *GROWLER* AFFAIR

One of the missions undertaken by Commander John G. Mitchell, commanding the USS *Saginaw*, was to learn whether the crew and passengers of the schooner *Growler* had been murdered by Indians or had drowned when the vessel was wrecked at or near Cape Chacon, the southern point of Prince of Wales Island.

The *Growler* was well known on Puget Sound where she had been built in 1858 at Oak Harbor, Whidbey Island, by John M. Izett for Captain Edward Barrington, Sr.[1] Captain Barrington was the father of three sons who made names for themselves as boatmen on the rivers of Yukon Territory and Alaska during the Klondike Rush and afterward.

Whether Barrington still owned the vessel in 1867 and 1868 is uncertain, but she was in command of Captain Horace Coffin in December 1867 when she became one of many vessels to visit the territory newly acquired from Russia. The *Growler* entered Customs at Sitka on December 26 and may have been under charter to Hayward M. Hutchinson, who was aboard her.[2]

Hutchinson had come north to purchase some of the immense inventory of the Russian-American Company and would soon form Hutchinson, Kohl & Company, which a few years later became the Alaska Commercial Company.

The *Growler* cleared from Sitka for San Francisco on January 21, 1868, with cargo consigned from Hutchinson & Hirsch to Sloss & Company. The manifest included 14 boxes, 10,537 lb., thick sheathing metal; 10 boxes, 3,076 lb., thin sheathing metal; 1 roll, 1,250 lb., sheet lead; 206 coils, 27,455 lb., cordage; 161 sheets, 23,150 lb., sheet copper; 45

pieces, 2,102 lb., zinc spelter; 39 pieces, 1,723 lb., tin; 12 pieces, 1,339 lb., tin; 63 bundles, 6,107 lb., calf skins (1,575 hides); 30 bundles, 3,389 lb., Russian leather (360 hides); 5 pieces, 2,511 lb., brass cannon; 8 pieces, 2,509 lb., brass bells; 32 bolts sail cloth; 1 box Russian iron.[3]

Presumably the *Growler* landed her cargo at San Francisco and probably loaded cargo there for Sitka as well. The Lewis and Dryden marine history said this about her last voyage:

> The traders of Vancouver and Queen Charlotte islands had always been confronted with a greater danger than shipwreck, and in 1868 the numerous outrages committed by Indians culminated in the murder of the entire crew of the Growler. The vessel left Victoria in March 1868 with a $35,000 cargo for the American Fur Company at Sitka and was wrecked off Cape Murray, Queen Charlotte Islands. None of her crew ever reached civilization again and their exact fate will always remain a mystery, although guarded statements of the natives years afterward proved that those who escaped death when the schooner was wrecked met a worse fate at the hands of the Hydah Indians.[4]

There is no Cape Murray on the Queen Charlotte Islands. It is the name used by early trading vessels for what is now Cape Chacon.

Just when word reached Sitka that the *Growler* had been wrecked is not known but the people there collected about $150 to send Charles Trueworthy to Cape Chacon to find bodies from the wreck, bring them to Sitka and to ascertain all he could about the wreck, according to word sent to Victoria, B.C., by Barney O'Regan.[5] That was the pen name of Thomas G. Murphy who later established the weekly *Alaska Times* at Sitka.

Barney O'Regan later reported to the *Colonist* that Trueworthy had returned to Sitka and had brought back a few silver coins and a pocket knife identified as belonging to Captain Coffin. "From his report it would seem practically impossible for any of the crew to have reached shore alive. It is certain that the lost schooner was the *Growler*, but the circumstances will probably never be known. Mr.

Trueworthy buried such remains as he found and marked the place of burial with headboards. Many bones were found in the woods, having doubtless been carried there by wolves."[6]

The earliest published report of the loss of the *Growler* may have been the one in the *Port Townsend Weekly Message* on May 7, 1868. The article said:

> The schooner *Growler*, Captain Horace Coffin, which sailed from Victoria on March 19 for Sitka, was lost with all hands near the entrance to Clarence Strait. Word was brought down by the *Otter* [the Hudson's Bay Company's steamer] which arrived at Victoria on April 19. The *Otter* was at Masset Harbor on April 9 and received word from the Indians who had returned from where evidence of the wreck was found, which was at Cape Murray, some 40 miles distant. The bodies of three men and a woman were found and a boat, some boxes of apples and two small kegs of liquor. From the body of one man the Indians took a specimen gold pin which was brought to Victoria by Captain Lewis and identified by the manufacturer as one belonging to one of the persons on board, known as Long John.
>
> The schooner had 20 tons of salt as ballast and a few other articles belonging to the owners of the vessel. The supposition is she was struck by a squall during the night, shifted cargo and either sank or drifted on a reef and broke up. The vessel and cargo were valued at $10,000, partly insured, and owned by the new American Fur Company and Captain Coffin.
>
> The captain was well and favorably known as Tom Coffin. He had been a long time in these waters and was the pilot for the Telegraph Company and also for our own men-of-war after the acquisition of the territory of Alaska. He was a native of Main and about 40 years old. Harris McAlmond [apparently the mate] was long a resident on the Sound and until recently lived at New Dungeness. He leaves a wife and children at Victoria.
>
> The other 11 people on board were George H. Nicol, Abraham Jackson, Thomas Riley, A. Steward, C. A. Timson, John Shephard, Samuel Thompson, a young man from San Francisco, name unknown, and two half-breed Natives, male and female.
>
> The *Growler* was a vessel of about 50 tons, neatly coppered and thoroughly repaired. There is a bare

possibility that some were saved but the general belief is that all perished.

The U.S. Consul at Victoria wrote that the *Growler* carried a mixed cargo of American and foreign goods valued at $35,000.[7]

Another report, published recently, says:

> The *Growler* left Victoria outfitted for sealing in the Pribilof Islands. The vessel was lost at sea with all aboard. Wreckage and bodies of the crew washed ashore on the south end of Prince of Wales Island. It was reported that all survivors were slain by Haida Indians.[8]

It was far too early in the season for a voyage to the Pribilofs, which could be locked in the ice pack until late May, so that was undoubtedly another wild guess.

While speculation appeared in print that the *Growler* capsized or foundered, apparently nobody guessed that she might, while running at night, simply have missed the entrance to Clarence Strait and crashed into the rocks at or near Cape Chacon while most of those aboard were below and asleep. The circumstances of the wreck are entirely guesswork.

The *Saginaw*, bound from San Francisco for Sitka with a stop at Victoria, B.C., left Victoria on April 29, the same day the *Otter* arrived from the north with news of the loss of the *Growler*. Thus Commander Mitchell would not have heard of that wreck until after he reached Sitka on May 7.

The *Saginaw* left Sitka on May 25, touched briefly at "Stachine" where the Army was building Fort Wrangell, then headed directly for Cape Chacon. As the ship neared the cape it overhauled three Indians in a canoe and Mitchell took one of them aboard to act as pilot to the wreck scene.

Commander Mitchell wrote from Sitka after his return there:

> After arriving at Cape de Chackan [*sic*] I got on board several of the Indians, one of whom had been living for a number of years in Victoria and had strong recommendations for his friendship to the Americans

and enquired very closely into the affair. "Ka-oun," the Indian to whom I referred above, told me that the wreck of the Schooner had been entirely broken up, but that her anchors and chains were still on shore.

I sent and brought them aboard. Further talk with the Indians satisfied me that the Indians of the "Kou" tribe were not the first to discover the wreck, that the Queen Charlotte Indians had plundered the wreck before the "Kous" knew anything. So I went over to Queen Charlotte and had a consultation with the Chief of the Masset tribe.

He acknowledged to his tribe having taken a considerable quantity of articles from the wreck, the principal part of which was Whiskey and other liquors, which had already been drank. No light was shown here, however, with regard to the murder of any of the people of the "Growler".

On our return to this port [Sitka], stopping at Stachine, one of the Indians, whom I brought as a passenger from Queen Charlotte, told the Squaw, who was kept by an American at that post [Stachine?], that the whole party were murdered by a party of Indians consisting of thirty (30) or more of the Noonagh [Hoonah] tribe headed by their chief "Steen-yah", and that the Chief and several of the Indians were wounded in the affair. This Indian said that he would, upon his arrival at this place, state the whole affair of the murder before the proper authorities.

On our arrival here, however, he refused to tell anything at all, and I am keeping him a prisoner on board until I can get the Chief down here from "Cross Sound" and the other witnesses from Stackine.

This party of "Hoonahs" passed through here on the 7th. inst. all dressed in cloth clothes. When they went down the coast they scarcely had a blanket apiece. "Steen-yah," the Chief, has a house here as well as at "Cross Sound".

I am going to pursue the investigation further as soon as we finish taking in coal, which I expect will be to-morrow.[9]

At Cape Chacon two kedge anchors were retrieved from the wreck. The *Saginaw* then steamed some eight miles north to Gardner Harbor where the ship's log reported an Indian village named "Retwoon." It may have been only a summer camp, but there another anchor and two pieces of chain from the wreck were retrieved.[10]

From Gardner Harbor the *Saginaw* steamed across Dixon Entrance and at 12:55 A.M. on June 1 anchored near the entrance to Masset Inlet. At 9 o'clock they entered the inlet and at 1:45 P.M. dropped anchor in Masset Harbor, "300 yards offshore opposite the second village." At the village they found several items from the wreck: a quadrant, part of a clock, a "magazine" and a ring. These were taken on board the ship.[11]

The *Saginaw* remained two more days in Masset Harbor, apparently because of thick and squally weather and when she left she had aboard one or two Masset people as what Mitchell was pleased to call "passengers." It seems doubtful that their going was purely voluntary.

From Masset the *Saginaw* steamed back to Gardner Harbor, then headed south and anchored "off the Indian village, between Cape Chacon and Point Nunez." The village undoubtedly was in what is now known as Nichols Bay but which was unnamed then. At one or both of these places Mitchell picked up additional "passengers" so that he had four aboard when he got back to Sitka on June 10.

On June 11 the *Saginaw*'s log had this entry: "2 P.M. Received two Indians on board to retain until further orders to give testimony in the case of the schooner *Growler.*"

The Sitka correspondent of the *British Colonist*, Barney O'Regan, wrote under date of June 17:

> The Saginaw brought back four Indians arrested on suspicion of having murdered some of the survivors [of the *Growler*]. They tell incredible, improbable and various stories and each tells a different story. They were taken aboard at Kli-garin, near the scene of the wreck.[12]

Another report came from Emil Teichmann who was in Sitka in 1868 representing a firm of fur dealers. He wrote:

> One of [two ships recently arrived in Sitka] was the warship *Saginaw*, which for the second time had visited the scene of the wreck of the *Growler* to investi-

> gate that catastrophe, and on this occasion brought back with it conclusive evidence that the crew of the schooner had been slain, when they landed, by the piratical natives. A number of Hyder [*sic*] Indians were prisoners on board the warship and were to be brought for trial before the general in command. In course of the investigations it had already been proved that practically the whole cargo of the *Growler* had been salvaged by the Indians and part of it had been sold to other tribes; in fact, a mass of goods and provisions had been found in the camps of the Cape Chacoum [*sic*] and Georgina Indians which must have come from the ill-fated ship. A compass and sextant and other nautical instruments which were of course of no value to the natives, had been recovered from the Indians by the captain of the war-ship. One of the life-boats of the *Growler* in an absolutely seaworthy state was found in a camp, and obviously, if the crew of the vessel had been able to save themselves in it, they would not have been attacked by the Indians.
>
> Besides this an Indian squaw who had been brought by the warship as a witness seemed to have declared when she was drunk that the schooner had run aground near the coast during a violent storm; that the crew had tried to reach shore in their boats but had been received with gun-fire from the natives and been driven back. Some were drowned in the breakers and the few who managed to get ashore were killed by the Indians.
>
> It is difficult to say whether this story was entirely reliable, but the general opinion was that the squaw had told the truth while half stupefied even though, when she was examined later, she tried to contradict her previous statement.[13]

What happened to the *Growler*'s people was never established for certain. There was no trial of any Natives before General Davis. For one thing, his authority extended only to court martials of military personnel. Non-military trials were before the Magistrate's Court at Sitka for minor offenses; in the U.S. District Court at Portland, Oregon, for major ones.

So far as any discovered record shows, Commander Mitchell did not carry his inquiry any further. When the *Saginaw* sailed south to Victoria in August she stopped briefly at the Indian villages of Kasaan on Prince of Wales Island and Masset, Queen Charlotte Islands, and the only purpose for these stops seems to have been to return "passengers." Kasaan was likely the home village of any people who had been taken from Cape Chacon to Sitka.

Notes

1. E. W. Wright, ed., *Lewis and Dryden's Marine History of the Pacific Northwest* (New York: Antiquarian Press, 1961), p. 94.

2. Richard A. Pierce, *Alaskan Shipping, 1867-1878: Arrivals and Departures at the Port of Sitka* (Kingston, Ontario: The Limestone Press, 1972), p. 6.

3. The ship's manifest in records of the U.S. Customs Service, Alaska Historical Library, Juneau.

4. E. W. Wright, ed., *op. cit.*, p. 168.

5. *British Colonist* (Victoria, B.C.), June 8, 1868.

6. *Ibid.*, June 17, 1868.

7. Allen Francis, U.S. Consul, report dated May 4, 1868.

8. Evert E. Tornfelt and Michael Burwell, *Shipwrecks of the Alaskan Shelf and Shore* (Anchorage: U.S. Dept. of the Interior, Minerals Management Service, Alaska OCS Region, 1992), p. 15.

9. Lt.-Commander John G. Mitchell to Rear Admiral H. K. Thatcher, Sitka, June 15, 1868, U.S. Navy, U.S.S. *Saginaw* Collection, Folder "Letters Received and Forwarded," pp. 70-72 (copy also available in typescript); Archives, Alaska and Polar Regions Department, Elmer E. Rasmuson Library, University of Alaska Fairbanks.

10. U.S. Department of the Navy, Records of the Bureau of Naval Personnel, Record Group 24, M/F 145, Roll 2, Log of the USS *Saginaw*, May 31, 1868. Archives, Alaska and Polar Regions Department, Elmer E. Rasmuson Library, University of Alaska Fairbanks.

11. Log of the USS *Saginaw*, June 1, 1868.

12. *British Colonist*, July 4, 1868.

13. Emil Teichmann, *A Journey to Alaska in the Year 1868* (New York: Argosy-Antiquarian, 1963), pp. 243-244.

III

FROM FORT WRANGELL TO SAN FRANCISCO

After Commander Mitchell's inconclusive quest for information about the crew and passengers of the *Growler*, the *Saginaw* anchored off Fort Wrangell at 8 P.M. on June 4. That was the first time the name was used in her log.

The weather was pleasant and for the next two days the crew was painting and cleaning the ship. On Sunday, June 7, the crew was mustered and the Articles of War were read. At 12 o'clock noon the battery ashore fired a 37-gun salute and the flag was raised for the first time over the new fort. That establishment was far from completed and still another fort was being built farther south. Captain C. H. Pierce, with another contingent from Company E of the 2nd Artillery, was building what would become Fort Tongass on the island of the same name. Both places would receive additional building materials, including 20,000 bricks for each fort, from Sitka in July.

In addition to the Army, the Treasury Department was now active at Fort Wrangell. C. C. Waldron, a trader, had been given a temporary appointment as Inspector of Customs at the port, and George Hamilton was putting up a building for a Customs office on a contract of $150 for his labor.

It seems probable that Commander Mitchell talked with Hamilton at Fort Wrangell and that Hamilton told him of a coal seam he had discovered in a bay on the northwest side of Kupreanof Island. Little is known about George Hamilton, although he has many descendants in Alaska. He was at Sitka for a time after the transfer and did some contract carpentry work for the city government.

He may have gone with the Army as a civilian employee to build Fort Wrangell. Later he established a salmon saltery at Hamilton's Fishery, the place today known as Klawock. Still later he was associated with Oliver Fontaine in a sawmill on Kosciusko Island at what was known as Hamilton's Mill until the Tlingit name Shakan was adopted for the place.

On June 9 the *Saginaw* sailed for Sitka with an overnight stop in Saginaw Bay, reaching Sitka at 7 P.M. on the 10th. "Seven passengers and their baggage left the ship," according to the log, but there is no indication who they were or where they came from. More than likely they were Army personnel from Fort Wrangell. The ship also "received on board two Indians to retain until further orders to give testimony in the case of the *Growler*." They undoubtedly were Indians the *Saginaw* had brought from Masset or Cape Chacon, or both.

There was some fine weather at Sitka this time and the crew did some painting as well as cutting wood and hauling water. The British schooner *Black Diamond* arrived from Nanaimo, B.C., with coal and the *Saginaw* took 21 tons from her and another 34 tons from a lighter.

There was some trouble ashore. On June 16 an officer was sent to bring back three men who were in the calaboose. Once aboard they were ordered confined in double irons for five days on bread and water. Four days later two of the crew, James Gordon and P. J. Frost, were arrested by the city constable and charged with burglary and robbery. They were tried in the Mayor's court, found guilty and sentenced to 18 months in jail. Their personal effects were sent ashore.

The bark *Delaware* arrived on June 23, 22 days from San Francisco, with government cargo and mail. From her and from the Army the *Saginaw* received three barrels of port, 500 pounds of flour, a barrel of sugar, 29 pieces of bacon, a sack of rice and a box of soap.

The *Saginaw* sailed on June 24 for Saginaw Bay where more surveys were made. From there she went to Kalahoo Bay, Kupreanof Island, "to obtain coal said to exist there." Commander Mitchell renamed the bay Hamilton Bay and it is known by that name today.

They spent three days at Hamilton Bay, digging and blasting coal from the narrow seam they found there. Commander Mitchell gave some details in a letter to Admiral H. K. Thatcher, USN, who commanded the North Pacific Squadron:

> At this point we found that Mr. Hamilton, who had been previously forward to prospect for coal, and left about a ton of coal on the beach. I sent a party ashore here, and worked out about 3 tons more.[1]

Commander Mitchell told the admiral that the fires had been started at 10:05 P.M. on July 1 and that steam was raised in one hour compared to 55 minutes for the Navarins coal they had been using. "This [Hamilton Bay] coal was merely the cropping taken without any selection and with the dirt and all among it, picked up by the sailors on the beach and was from a vein about 18 in. thick," Mitchell wrote to the admiral. He added, "Besides the coal there is every evidence of *Petroleum* in considerable quantity on the island."[2]

Despite Commander Mitchell's "every evidence," no petroleum has yet been found on the islands of Southeastern Alaska.

In his letter to Admiral Thatcher he gave the Hamilton coal high marks, reporting a speed of nine and a half knots a five-hour run, with only four of the six furnaces in use.

The *Saginaw* arrived back at Saginaw Bay in the evening on July 1. The next day was spent in painting and surveying and on July 3 they were engaged in "exercising the boats and guns and drilling at repelling boarders."

On the Fourth of July they dressed ship and had a four-mile race between the 2nd and 3rd cutters, each pulling five oars. The 2nd cutter won by one minute. The ship left the bay at noon, as Commander Mitchell reported in his letter to Admiral Thatcher:

> From Saginaw Bay we sailed on the 4th of July for Kastznoo [Kootznahoo] (see tracing) and finding the anchorage bad in front of the village, ran in behind the little Island shewing on the chart, anchoring in 9 fms water: this is a very snug anchorage. We had come up to this point to look at and try some coal said to exist and of which an Indian had brought some fine specimens.[3]

He did not say where the Indian had taken the specimens but it was probably close to Sitka.

On Sunday, July 5, it was foggy and the *Saginaw* remained at anchor behind Killisnoo Island all day. There was some trouble aboard. During the second dog watch, 6 to 8 P.M., "John Ponte, mate, placed under arrest per Commanding Officer for insolence to the executive officer, until further orders." Forty-eight hours later he was "released from arrest temporarily by order of Commander."

That arrest and temporary release may have had something to do with Ponte's subsequent employment as a coal miner.

The *Saginaw* entered Kootznahoo Inlet (there is a variety of spellings in the log), found the coal and spent four days getting some of it. The entire coal endeavor, however, stretched out into the ship's second Alaska voyage, under Commander Meade, and is detailed in Chapter 7.

At 4:30 P.M. on July 9 the *Saginaw* again dropped anchor at Sitka. The next days were devoted to taking aboard water and wood but on Saturday the 11th there was an excursion trip: "At 10:15 A.M. stood out. Passed Kulik Reef at 11:45. At 1:05 anchored at a fishing station at Klutchoo Lake. At 6:45 stood for Sitka. Anchored at 8:40." That could only have been a trip to the Redoubt but the log gives no clue as to whether any Sitka people were included.

The ship took on "stores" that had arrived on the mail steamer *George S. Wright* and a quantity of lumber and some tools for the coal mining operation at Kootznahoo Inlet. On July 17 the American ship *Winged Arrow* arrived in the harbor and soon afterward, according to the log: "Sent the 3rd cutter to tow to Government Island [Japonski?] a scow with 10 head of cattle for ship's use." No doubt Michael Graham, 28 and born in Ireland, would have opportunities to exercise his skills. His rating aboard the *Saginaw* was 2nd class fireman but when he enlisted his occupation was listed as "butcher."

A reward of $20 apiece was offered for the return of four deserters and by that evening they were back aboard the ship. Whether the reward was collected was not stated. Mate William Kneeland resigned and left the ship.

On July 18 the *Saginaw* towed the bark *Delaware* to sea, then went through Peril Strait, stopped for 15 minutes off Kootznahoo village and went on to Saginaw Bay where they remained for only an hour. At midnight they were in Frederick Sound where the log reported "large quantities of floating ice."

Fog was encountered in Wrangell Narrows but the ship proceeded at slow speed "with both leads going and anchor ready to let go." There was a strong head tide a part of the way and it was necessary to run the engines at full speed to stem it but the ship got through without mishap and anchored at Fort Wrangell.

Two days later the ship steamed down Clarence Strait and at 3:55 P.M. on July 22nd it rounded Grindall Island and headed for the Indian village of "Casaan." An officer was sent ashore to learn where the principal chief could be found. The ship then steamed up the inlet to a settlement "15 miles above Cape Grindall." That would appear to have been Karta Bay but although a blank cartridge was fired from a howitzer, so far as the log shows, neither the principal chief nor anyone else responded.

From Kasaan Bay the *Saginaw* steamed to Fort Tongass where she found HMS survey ship *Beaver* and the *George S. Wright* at anchor. After stopping there for an hour and a half, the *Saginaw* went around to Fort Simpson on the Canadian side of the border. She spent two hours there before returning to Fort Tongass.

Neither the log book nor Commander Mitchell's letters give any indication what that activity was about but it seems likely that the *Growler* wreck was still under investigation.

The *Saginaw* left Fort Tongass early in the morning on July 23. At 6 P.M. Ensign Vail, the watch officer, wrote in the log that Mary Island was abeam, and at 8:30 P.M. Mate John Ponte wrote that they were entering Tongass Narrows.

Where did they get those names? Undoubtedly they came from Pilot Robert Hicks. The *Dictionary of Alaska Place Names* says that Mary Island was named in 1880 and Tongass Narrows about 1878-1880, but obviously the names were in use long before those dates.

The *Saginaw* made brief stops at Fort Wrangell and Saginaw Bay, then went into Kootznahoo Inlet for work on the coal project and to take aboard some of the coal. When she left Kootznahoo Inlet she headed up Chatham Strait and Lynn Canal on July 30, making her first visit to that area. She entered Lynn Canal at 2 A.M. and at 9 o'clock, according to the log, "stopped an hour and a half off Sullivan Island to take on board the stores and tackle and five men of the schooner *Louisa Downs* which was wrecked on the island."

The skipper of the wrecked schooner was Michael Sullivan and Commander Mitchell undoubtedly then and there named the island for him. The *Dictionary of Alaska Place Names*, however, says: "Named by Comdr. R. W. Meade, USN, for the master of the American schooner *Louisa Downs* which was wrecked on the island in 1867." Wrong man and wrong year.

The story of the *Louisa Downs* is something of a puzzle. The 45-foot, two-masted schooner had first arrived in Sitka in the summer of 1867, probably with freight and passengers from Victoria. She went south a month later and did not return to Sitka until June 1868 when she hailed from Port Townsend in command of Michael Sullivan. On June 20 she cleared "for a trading and prospecting voyage southeast of Sitka to Tarkou and Stikine rivers."[4]

The manifest of trading goods carried by the *Louisa Downs* on the voyage:

124	gallons molasses	$40.66
14	barrels flour	75.00
2	pieces cotton cloth	16.12
2	boxes tobacco	16.80
1	dozen rings &	
15	sets jewelry	9.00
1	box pipes and rings	7.00
12	lb. gunpowder	6.00
6	bottles whiskey	18.00
2	doz. shirts	18.00
6	pieces calico	26.15
3	boxes bread	26.28
5½	doz. handkerchiefs	13.75
60	yards blue cloth	9.00
1	doz. soap	1.25
	Sundry trade goods	75.00
50	lb. shot	5.00

The gunpowder, shot and whiskey were carried only with the special permission of General Jefferson Davis as their sale in Alaska was restricted.[5] The total value of the manifest was $363.01. How much of it was taken aboard the *Saginaw* at Sullivan Island was not reported.

The *Saginaw*, according to her log, took aboard not only the stores but the tackle — anchors, chain, sails, rigging — and her crew of five. She was stripped, and abandoned.

Despite that, the *Louisa Downs* was back in Sitka two months later and on September 22 was issued a new document at the Customs House. It changed her registry from Port Angeles, W.T., to Sitka, but it did not reveal who salvaged the vessel from Sullivan Island or how that was done. So far as is known, that story was never reported in print. The salvor may have been Captain Henry Hanson who was listed in the new document as one of her owners. The other was J. M. Manasse, a Sitka merchant.

The *Louisa Downs*, in charge of Captain Hanson, cleared from Sitka on October 12, 1868, on another trading voyage. After touching at several Indian villages she sailed out past Cape Spencer and up the coast but was dismasted in a gale and drifted ashore at or near Dry Bay on November 22. Hanson and his two crew members got back to Sitka but not until the following June. And this time the *Louisa Downs* stayed on the beach, a total loss.

After leaving Sullivan Island the *Saginaw* continued up Lynn Canal for nearly four hours. That could have put her well up into Taiya Inlet, but it is uncertain where she anchored for the night. She left that anchorage at 4:10 A.M. on July 31 and anchored that night in Freshwater Bay, Chichagof Island. The following day the vessel was stopped off Kutznahoo Inlet and Mate John Ponte went ashore to oversee the coal mining operations. He had 400 board feet of lumber to build a shelter and a Sharps carbine for protection, if needed.

The next stop was Sitka where the *Saginaw* took aboard stores and coal during a three-day stay. It would be Commander Mitchell's last visit to Sitka although he had not planned it that way.

On August 5 the *Saginaw* went to the coal mine on Kootznahoo Inlet, dropping anchor there at 8:45 P.M. During the next two days she took aboard 444 sacks of Kootznahoo coal. During the afternoon of August 6 there was a significant entry in the ship's deck log: "Placed three Indians in double irons by order of Commanding Officer for creating trouble on shore."

That would seem to indicate that the three Indians were on board the ship, perhaps by invitation, when seized. That is the only indication in the log of any kind of trouble with the Indians. And the three were not again mentioned in the log until December 22 when the *Saginaw*, by then in charge of Commander R. W. Meade, was "at Kootsnow village to land three (3) Indians carried off by Commander J. G. Mitchell."

By then the Indians had been aboard the *Saginaw* for more than four months and had been to Victoria, San Francisco and the Mare Island Navy Yard. There is little doubt that the Indians had been taken as hostages to insure the safety of Mate John Ponte at the coal mine. P. Meigs, clerk for Commander Meade, would write in his diary on December 22: "We stopped at Koutsnow this morning to leave the three Indian hostages, held for Mr. Ponti, Capt. Mitchell's clerk, who was left here some months ago."[6]

From Kootznahoo the *Saginaw* headed south, made brief stops at Saginaw Bay and Fort Wrangell, and at 6:45 A.M. on Sunday, August 9, she was heading for "Casaan" Harbor. At 9:45 A.M. the ship "laid to at the fishing station 6 miles to westward of Cape Grindall." Then at 2:15 "arrived off the Indian village. At 3:00 started ahead."

Why did Commander Mitchell go to the old Haida village of Kasaan on this trip? We can only surmise that it was to drop off one of the men he had carried north to Sitka in June to provide information about the wreck of the *Growler*.

There was a surprise entry at 3:15 P.M. on the 9th, a Sunday: "Held divine services on the quarterdeck, Chaplain Raynor, USA, presiding."

Chaplain Raynor had presumably boarded the *Saginaw* at Sitka. He had arrived there with the Army in 1867 and remained for two years before being transferred to another post. With him at Sitka was a son, Frank W. Raynor, who worked as a clerk in the Custom House until the fall of 1869 when he resigned to go south with his father.

But on this trip, in August 1868, Chaplain Raynor must have been on leave of absence from his post at Sitka, going south to Victoria and probably continuing beyond Victoria. The ship's deck log gives no indication just when Commander Mitchell decided it would be necessary to take his ship to Victoria for repairs, but it appears to have been at least as early as her most recent visit to Sitka and that Chaplain Raynor boarded her because she was going to Victoria.

A major reason for the needed repairs was the use of Kootznahoo coal, although neither the ship's deck log nor Commander Mitchell's letters stated that fact. But Commander Richard Worsam Meade, who succeeded Mitchell in command of the *Saginaw*, put his fist squarely on the problem in two letters to Admiral T. T. Craven. In one letter he said:

> The Koutsnow coal used by Commander J. G. Mitchell is not suitable for steamers. It is too volatile, contains too great a quantity of resin, heats the smokestack red hot at its lower joint and is liable to spontaneous combustion. I regard it as dangerous.[7]

Earlier, after he had examined the engine room log of the *Saginaw* at Mare Island, Meade wrote:

> On July 21, 1868, the woodwork around the steam drum took fire. On August 5 at 1:40 P.M. the woodwork again took fire and the same on August 7 at 4 P.M. and 10:30 P.M.
>
> On August 8 the smokestack was so hot that the log states a stream of water was played on it.

The entry "woodwork on fire" occurs on August 9, 10 and 11 and on the latter date there is the entry "discontinued using this (Koutsnow) coal."[8]

August 9, one of the days on which the woodwork in the engine room caught fire, was the day the *Saginaw* left Kasaan Bay and headed down Clarence Strait. She did not stop at Fort Tongass and on the 10th, when she was crossing Dixon Entrance, there was another engine room fire. The third fire listed by Commander Meade occurred on the 11th. The ship entered Massett Inlet at 5:30 in the morning and dropped anchor soon afterward.

Why did the *Saginaw* stop at Massett? It can only be presumed that it was to return another of the Indians who had been taken away earlier in the year in connection with the *Growler* inquiry.

Immediately after the anchor was down at Massett "the engineers blowed down the port boiler" and started work on it. The repairs were completed at 11:25, steam was raised and the *Saginaw* moved out of the harbor at 1:20 P.M. That was the day they ceased using the Kootznahoo coal, according to Commander Meade's letter.

The *Saginaw* rounded Rose Point and stood down Hecate Strait toward Victoria where she dropped anchor in the harbor at 5:40 P.M. on August 13. The next day the ship was hauled alongside a dock and the smokestack lifted out, after which she returned to an anchorage. The ship was at Victoria for 27 days and on every day except the four Sundays workmen came from shore each morning and spent the day on board. There were carpenters who undoubtedly were replacing the burned woodwork and perhaps doing other jobs. There were mechanics who for the most part "worked on the wheels" but sometimes "did other work about the ship." There is no indication in the log whether the work on the paddle wheels was routine maintenance or whether they had been damaged during the voyage. And on some days the work gangs included locksmiths, for unspecified work.

On August 31 Commander Mitchell wrote to Admiral Craven:

> I am still detained here by repairs on the machinery and wheels. . .; but it looks now as though there is some chance of leaving here during the present week.
>
> The work ought to have been finished sooner, but for the great scarcity of machinists and black smiths.
>
> I have been very impatient to get away especially since the news has reached here of the boarding and robbing of the English schooner "Black Diamond" by a party of the Henega tribe of Indians some 80 miles from Sitka.
>
> This is one of the (3) three tribes of Indians in Inland waters that I have not visited. But for the "Suwanee" failing us I should have gone through them also [a reference to the wreck of that Navy vessel in British Columbia on July 9, 1868, while bound for Alaska.]
>
> I have made it a point to stop at every place where there was even a village however small on my passages to and from the different points in our possessions North.
>
> The tribes yet to be visited are the Takus, Hoonahs of Cross Sound, and the Hanegas, which will receive my immediate attention.[9]

Commander Mitchell's statement that he had stopped "at every place where there was even a village, however small" is an exaggeration. In 1868 there were many Indian villages, some of only three or four houses, in the areas traversed by the *Saginaw*.

In another letter to Admiral Craven from Victoria, Commander Mitchell complained that only greenbacks — paper money — were being received at Sitka to pay the crew, although he had understood that specie would be provided. Greenbacks, he said, were discounted from 3 to 5 per cent in Sitka. In addition, the officers had to buy fish and meat from the Indians for their mess. "The Indians do not know what paper money is," he wrote. "They say, on looking at it, that they can get similar papers from cans of preserved fruit, vegetables, oysters, any can, in fact."[10]

During the 27 days the *Saginaw* was at Victoria, many of her crew were given shore leave, and there were many desertions. On August 18, for example, the log had this entry: "Offered to the authorities ashore $20 each for the return of nine deserters and $10 for one straggler." The result was the return, the following day, of one $20 man and the straggler. Several of the other deserters were returned later.

On September 2, B. Nelson was returned after overstaying his leave and was placed in double irons. That night, because the ship was so shorthanded, the leg irons were removed and he was placed on anchor watch. The next morning the log had a notation: "Missing, B. Nelson with irons, one pair." Had he jumped overboard and swum ashore while still in handcuffs? He was not returned on board and the question is unanswered.

At last the repairs were completed and the stores all aboard and at 5:50 on September 9 the *Saginaw* steamed out of the harbor bound for Alaska. She had barely cleared the harbor when there was an engine breakdown and she drifted while repairs were being made. As she drifted a dispatch boat came out with a telegram for Commander Mitchell. It ordered him to take his ship to San Francisco. Only the engine breakdown had made delivery of the telegram possible and its delivery would prove inopportune for five of the men aboard. One was Commander Mitchell and another was a passenger, the Alaskan Mikhail Kadin. They had been headed back north but because of the telegram neither would see Alaska again. The other three were the Indian hostages from Kootznahoo. They would eventually get back to Alaska but their return to their homes was delayed by nearly three months.

The *Saginaw* dropped anchor in San Francisco Bay at 7:30 A.M. on September 15.

NOTES

1. Lt.-Commander John G. Mitchell to Rear Admiral H. K. Thatcher, Sitka, July 10, 1868, U.S. Navy, U.S.S. *Saginaw* Collection, Folder "Letters Received and Forwarded," pp. 73-77 (copy also available in typescript); Archives, Alaska and Polar Regions Department, Elmer E. Rasmuson Library, University of Alaska Fairbanks).

2. *Ibid.*

3. *Ibid.*

4. Richard A. Pierce, *Alaskan Shipping, 1867-1878: Arrivals and Departures at the Port of Sitka* (Kingston, Ontario: The Limestone Press, 1972), p. 11.

5. Records of the Sitka Custom House, in the Alaska Historical Library, Juneau.

6. Diary of Peveril Meigs. See Chapter 4.

7. Richard W. Meade to T. T. Craven, commanding the North Pacific Squadron, Sitka, December 26, 1868. From R. W. Meade Letterbook, 1868-69, p. 10. On microfilm from New York Historical Society.

8. From Mare Island, California, November 27, 1868, Meade Letterbook, *op. cit.*, p. 6.

9. Lt.-Commander John G. Mitchell to Rear Admiral Thomas T. Craven, Victoria, V.I., August 31, 1868, U.S. Navy, U.S.S. *Saginaw* Collection, Folder "Letters Received and Forwarded," pp. 68-69 (copy also available in typescript); Archives, Alaska and Polar Regions Department, Elmer E. Rasmuson Library, University of Alaska Fairbanks.

10. Lt.-Commander John G. Mitchell to Rear Admiral Thomas T. Craven, Victoria, V.I., August 22, 1868, U.S. Navy, U.S.S. *Saginaw* Collection, Folder "Letters Received and Forwarded," pp. 65-67 (copy also available in typescript); Archives, Alaska and Polar Regions Department, Elmer E. Rasmuson Library, University of Alaska Fairbanks.

IV

INTERLUDE

The USS *Saginaw*, back from Alaska, anchored off San Francisco on Tuesday morning, September 15, 1868. The crew was kept busy all day cleaning the ship. In the afternoon, 4th Assistant Engineer James Godfrey reported for duty. He would remain in the ship for her second Alaska voyage but 3rd Assistant Engineer F. Skeel, who reported aboard the following day, remained for only a couple of weeks, probably to assist with engine repairs. Crew member L. Larkin left the ship without permission in the evening on the 15th. Desertions would be fairly frequent during the two months and a half the *Saginaw* was at San Francisco and the Mare Island Navy Yard.

On Wednesday they dressed ship in honor of the anniversary of the independence of Mexico and on Friday they strung up the flags again to honor the independence of the Republic of Chile. The crew did some cleaning and painting and on Sunday at 4:20 P.M. the ship got under way for Mare Island. It was necessary to drop anchor twice because of thick fog and they did not make fast to a buoy off the Navy Yard until 1:15 P.M. on Monday.

On September 23 a survey party boarded the ship from the Navy Yard to inspect the engines. This was the first of four parties of officers from the Navy Yard who would inspect the ship during the next several weeks.

Four new crew members arrived aboard from the receiving ship *Independence* and two of the men who had made the Alaska trip signed up for three more years when their enlistments expired.

During the seven and a half weeks the *Saginaw* was at Mare Island, workmen, including painters, caulkers, carpenters, boilermakers and mechanics from the Navy Yard boarded her nearly every day. She was drydocked overnight so a piece of sheet copper, lost in one of her strandings in Alaska, could be replaced. Gunpowder and cartridges were moved to a magazine ashore; her sails were unbent and stored and the yards and topmasts sent down and scraped. Much of the rigging was replaced. The two holds were emptied, washed and painted. The officers shifted their quarters to the USS *Jamestown* and the enlisted men to the *Vanderbilt* for several days while their quarters were being cleaned and painted but returned to the *Saginaw* each morning to resume work.

On October 11 Commander Mitchell, who apparently had been staying ashore and perhaps in San Francisco, inspected the ship.

During the forenoon watch on Thursday, October 22, Midshipman E. W. Bridge, newly arrived aboard, made this entry in the log: "Received telegram from San Francisco announcing the death of our commanding officer, Lieut.-Commander John G. Mitchell."

The *New York Times* on October 23 carried an item dated from San Francisco on the 21st:

> Captain Mitchell, commander of the United States steamer Saginaw, was murdered tonight at the corner of Stockton and Sutter streets in the very heart of the city. The body was robbed.

An official report of the death was made to Admiral T. T. Craven, commanding the North Pacific Squadron, by Captain J. M. Frailey of the USS *Saranac* on October 26:

> I regret to report the death, on the evening of October 21st of Lieut Comdr. John G. Mitchell late of the 'Saginaw', who was murdered in San Francisco on the evening of that day by two (2) men who have since been arrested and are now in prison.
>
> The body of Lieut Commander Mitchell was deposited in the Cemetery, on Mare Island, on Saturday afternoon Oct. 24th., by a Masonic and Naval funeral.[1]

The *Alaska Herald*, published in San Francisco, had this information: "Captain Mitchell was in hopes to be able to return to Alaska next spring. He had been relieved of the command of the *Saginaw* and ordered East . . . He also contemplated organizing a company to work a coal mine at Cook's Inlet that he discovered in his late cruise."[2] The story is, of course, in error as to the location of the coal discovery. Its other information may have been more accurate.

John Gardner Mitchell was born in Massachusetts and in 1856 graduated from the Naval Academy at Annapolis, where he was a classmate of Richard W. Meade who succeeded him in command of the *Saginaw*. He served with the Pacific Squadron, then with the Coast Survey, and was an instructor at the Naval Academy when the Civil War began. He served with the Mississippi River Squadron, then was called to the Ordinance Department in Washington. After the war ended he returned to the Pacific Squadron and was given command of the *Saginaw* with which he patrolled the coast both north and south of California. Mitchell Bay in Kootznahoo Inlet, Admiralty Island, Alaska, was named for Commander Mitchell by his classmate, Richard Worsam Meade.

Aboard the *Saginaw* the executive officer, Acting Master C. C. Bunker, took command for two days. Then Ensign A. H. Vail was listed in the daily log as the commanding officer until November 2 when Lieut.-Commander Lester A. Beardslee took command.

In all the time since August 6 when they were brought aboard there was no mention in the ship's deck log of the three Indians who had been brought aboard in double irons. Were they kept in confinement? Were they, with the crew, transferred to the *Vanderbilt* while work was being done on the *Saginaw*? No answers have been found to those questions, but information provided later at Sitka, it is apparent that one of the prisoners, known as Jake, was on good terms with the ship's officers. (See the Meigs diary for January 12, 1869, in Chapter 6.) And we know from something Commander Beardslee wrote many years later that the Indians were still aboard the *Saginaw* while he was her commanding officer.

In 1879 Commander Beardslee was sent to Sitka with the USS *Jamestown* and remained in Sitka for 15 months. In August 1880 he visited a number of Indian villages to talk with the chiefs and he wrote this of his stop at Kootznahoo:

> Our interview with the Indians was held on the 17th, it having been necessary to send for a leading chief to a salmon river, some 25 miles away. This chief, Kitchnath (Jake), was one of the Indians who were, in 1868, carried away as hostages by Lieutenant Commander Mitchell in the Saginaw, and I found him a prisoner when I assumed command of that vessel at Mare Island. My treatment of him and the other Indian prisoners on the Saginaw was fortunately such that as soon as Jake recognized me he was ready to comply with all that I should ask. The other chief, Grandshana (Andrew), had a most excellent letter from Lieutenant Commander (now Captain) Meade, and from all I can learn of him he has continued to deserve it.[3]

The name of the third Indian prisoner has not been established.

On November 6 Mate John Ponte rejoined the *Saginaw* at Marc Island. In August he had been left at Kootznahoo Inlet to work the coal mine there with a crew of Indians. After all the coal sacks were filled, Ponte was taken to Sitka in an Indian canoe and from there he traveled to San Francisco in the Revenue Cutter *Wayanda*. He stood a regular watch aboard the *Saginaw* until November 18 when he was detached and ordered to the receiving ship *Independence*.

At 12:15 P.M. on November 11 the *Saginaw* cast off from the buoy at Mare Island and at 3 o'clock dropped anchor off San Francisco. The following day the ship began receiving fresh water and stores, including fresh beef and vegetables and furniture for the cabin and wardroom. Additional crew members were received from the *Independence* and were exercised with muskets and carbines and put to the task of bending sails.

On November 20 Lieut.-Commander Richard W. Meade boarded the ship. At 11:20 all hands were called on deck, Commander Beardslee was relieved and Commander Meade took command of the ship.

Commander Meade was born in New York in 1837, the son of Captain Richard Worsam Meade, USN, and Clara Meigs Meade. He went to the Naval Academy at age 13 and six years later, four of them spent at sea, graduated in 1856. He was promoted to lieutenant two years later but in 1860 was court-martialed and reprimanded for calling a Marine Corps lieutenant "a liar and a coward." When the Civil War broke out he was serving in the Pacific Squadron and was invalided home with fever in August 1861. He served as an ordnance instructor and briefly in two warships before being promoted to lieutenant commander on July 14, 1862, and given command of the *Louisville* on the Mississippi River. His next command was the *Marblehead* on the Charleston blockade. He was commended by Admiral John Dahlgren for his action against shore batteries during which his ship was hulled 30 times during a two-hour bombardment. His next command, until the end of the war was the *Chocura* in the Gulf of Mexico. Two months after the war ended Meade married Rebecca Paulding, the daughter of Admiral Hiram Paulding. From the summer of 1865 until early autumn of 1868 Meade was head of the seamanship department at Annapolis and during that time he published "Manual of the Boat Exercise at the U.S. Naval Academy" and "A Treatise on Naval Architecture." From Annapolis he was ordered to San Francisco to take command of the *Saginaw*. Seaton Schroeder, who as a midshipman served under Meade in the *Saginaw* and who rose to the rank of admiral, later described Meade as "a daring and skillful seaman but disconcertingly frank in both look and spoken expression whenever any one incurred his displeasure or failed to meet his professional expectations."[4]

If the story in the *Alaska Herald* was correct, Commander Meade may have been aware, even before Commander Mitchell's death, that he would command the *Saginaw* on another Alaska voyage. At any rate, sometime before October 24 he sent a telegram to his cousin, Peveril Meigs, inviting him to become the captain's clerk for the voyage. Meigs accepted.

Meigs was then 21. Two years earlier a coasting accident near his home at New Brighton, Staten Island, had necessitated surgery on one of his legs and had kept him bedridden for nearly a year. Still in a somewhat discouraged state of mind, he welcomed the invitation from San Francisco which he reached on November 16 after traveling by steamer via the Isthmus of Panama.

On November 20 Meigs moved aboard the *Saginaw* with his cousin and shared a cabin with him during the Alaska voyage. He kept a diary while on board and from it we have a much more detailed account of happenings during the voyage than we have of the voyage under Commander Mitchell. In the following chapters extracts from the diary will be identified with the prefix "Meigs." In the diary Meigs refers to his cousin, Commander Meade, as "Dick."

Commander Meade was not entirely pleased with conditions aboard the *Saginaw* when he took command. In a letter to the commanding officer of the Mare Island Navy Yard he wrote:

> I find upon assuming command that there are but three midshipmen on board for duty as watch officers. I request that two more be assigned temporarily until the vessel falls in with Rear Admiral Craven. I request that E. W. Bridge and Seaton Schroeder be the two assigned.[5]

Nor was Commander Meade satisfied with the *Saginaw*'s galley. On November 27 he wrote:

> The galley has an old-fashioned wood burning affair much too small for the requirements of the vessel unless a stove is provided for the officers' mess. If a coal burning galley stove to cook for 100 men were provided we could stow at least four weeks additional provisions.[6]

No indication has been found that either the additional stove for the officers' mess or the coal burning stove was provided.

The *Saginaw*'s log during the time she was anchored off San Francisco contains little except reports on the weather, notations of stores being received, and routine activities of the crew, but the Meigs diary goes into more detail of life aboard ship:

"Nov. 21st, Sat. We left the Occidental today and went on board the 'Saginaw'. Was made acquainted with the officers and find them all real jolly. Dick went to spend Sunday with a Mr. Ralston, one of the most influential men in 'Frisco' so I take possession of the cabin alone. Went ashore after writing some letters for the Capt'n, with the boy 'Jackson' to buy some things and returned at 5 o'clock. I am invited very kindly to mess in the Wardroom with the officers, and, as I cannot start our mess until tomorrow, accept. Find in the evening that two or three of them play on the flute so I get both of mine out and we have some duetts, trios, etc. They all seem quite musical and we sing and blow until I am hoarse. I unpacked my trunk soon after I came on board and Jackson stowed my things away for me. Find there is only one stateroom in the cabin, so I shall have a cot or hammock swung. Turned in about ten o'clock in Dick's stateroom and had another dream about home."

The only Jackson on the ship's muster roll was Joseph Jackson whose rating was Ordinary Seaman. He was 21, born in Harper's Ferry, Virginia, a mariner by trade, stood 5 feet 4½ inches and had a fair complexion.[7] Possibly he was acting as captain's steward until they went to sea.

Meigs: "Nov. 22nd, Sun. Wake up and find instead of being on Staten I'd I am afloat in the 'Saginaw' and a horrible scraping, rubbing, etc. going on over my head, enough to wake the dead. Have quarters at 10 A.M. and go to church for the first time since leaving home. Go to Grace Church and hear a splendid service, music elegant. Return on board at one P.M. My stores did not come off last night, so at 5 o'clock I take dinner in the Wardroom.

Have a little music in the cabin with the executive officer, Mr. Vail and am now going to turn in hoping to dream of home, *etc.* 3 bells.

"Nov. 23rd, Mon. Dick returned on board this morning and, after 'general quarters' I went on shore and saw to the stores and marketing. Grapes are about 5 cents a pound; they are small but taste something like Black Hamburgs. At the Navy's Agency I got a jolly long letter from Jim Pratt which made my heart rejoice. Dick got a letter from his wife which brought tears to his eyes, something I thought he was never guilty of. I must say that I could hardly see to read *mine* from some strange cause, for I do love to hear from *dear* old Staten Island. The drills with the guns and side arms amuse me considerably. The 'Saginaw' has six guns, two 30 lb. rifles, and four 24 lb. howitzers. The engine is undergoing some repairs, so that we will not leave here for a week or more. Dick is asleep on the lounge. He has just written to his wife and, I think, is a little homesick.

"Nov. 24th. Did not sleep well last night for I slept on the transom and felt as though I was rolling off all the time. I am going to have a hammock, or 'hang-up' as [my aunt] Katie calls it, slung in the cabin tonight so I hope to sleep better hereafter. I went ashore today and bought a pillow and some other necessary articles. Had a little music in the Wardroom and am now about to retire to the arms of that dear old fellow Morpheus.

"Nov. 25th, Wed. I commenced a letter to Jim Pratt yesterday and intended to finish it this morning, but Mr. Bridge insisted on my going ashore with him, so I went. We had some billiards, *etc.*, and I came on board at one o'clock and finished Jim's letter. I did full justice to the hammock last night; it is the first time I ever slept in one. Dick and I hung some small pictures around the cabin this afternoon. I put one where I could lie in my hammock and look at it. Dear little Angel [Rosamond Weston whom Meigs would marry in 1875].

"Nov. 26th, Thanksgiving Day. Wrote a letter to Katie. Sent Jim's and Katie's letters. Went with Dick to Grace Church and had the pleasure of sitting alongside a jolly young lady. I lent her my prayer book so she knows my name. I enjoyed it immensely, (I mean the sermon.) Saw a scull race and came aboard about 2 P.M. Capt. Greene took dinner with us. Had some champagne with the officers in the ward room; drank to *the one* absent. Left Mr. Bridge in an excess of ------ *good humor*. Dick did not come aboard until near ten o'clock, so I tumbled into my 'hang-up' without waiting for him.

"Nov. 27th, Fri. Sent a letter to Carrie Cook, also one to Father. Received stores on board. A schooner came foul of us this morning, and when the Capt. got on deck he ordered, 'Silence there, fore and aft. Cut everything that fouls!', which seemed to please the men *hugely*. One of them, the Coxswain of the Gig, said to me afterwards, 'Damn it, I would have cut away his bowsprit if Capt. Meade had only said so!', but fortunately there was no use for the axes. Staid up quite late and wrote to Louise.

"Nov. 28th, Sat. Sent Father's and Louise's letters, went ashore and bought powder, shot, etc. The 'Resaca' and 'Monongo' came in this morning and anchored quite near us. We expected Mr. and Mrs. Kellogg on board today but were disappointed. I forgot to say that Mr. Hobbs dined with us yesterday. The repairs to the machinery are about completed this evening and we expect to leave here on Monday. Wrote to Jim Truslow.

"Nov. 29th, Sun. Dick and I went to Grace Church this morning and enjoyed it very much; the young damsel in blue, that sat next to me on Thanksgiving Day, was there again and I cast sheep's-eyes at her all the time. Answered a letter of Mother's and wrote to Miss. Taylor, (Blackeyes.)"

Early in the forenoon watch on November 30, according to the ship's log, the boilers were filled and fire started to get up steam. Before noon received on board $10,683.39 in specie to freight to Sitka. At 2:25 the anchor was raised and at 2:45 the ship started out of the harbor in charge of a pilot but turned back because of heavy seas on the bar. Gave tow to a small schooner which capsized and sank, but the crew was saved. Came to anchor again at 4 P.M., after which Mrs. Kinkead and servant arrived on board for passage to Sitka, by order of Commodore Allen.

Meigs: "Nov. 30, Mon. Today has been one of intense excitement. I was busy all the morning on shore, brought the Russian Consul on board with some specie that Dick is going to take to Sitka for him. We got under way about 3 P.M. and on reaching the Bar found a fearful sea running and often breaking. We got a short distance on the Bar, but at last a sea broke right over us, and caused Dick to change his mind and wait until flood tide tomorrow when probably there will be less sea, so we turned back and are now peacefully at anchor somewhere near Meiggs Wharf. As we came through the Golden Gate we saw a small boat with the ensign reversed and a coat at the top of his foremast, a boat about 25 or 30 feet long, and running down to her we found there were three men on her, or rather boys, and none of them seeming to understand how to manage her. They were nearly out to the breakers, and but for our opportune arrival, the strong ebb tide would soon have sent them to Davy Jones' Locker. After much confusion we took her in tow, two of the men coming aboard the 'Saginaw' and one remaining to steer the boat. She came within an ace of capsizing several times, and at last *did* go over and filled; the foremast instantly was snapped out of her and she was left astern. The ship was stopped and the gig lowered, but before anything more was done, the boat disappeared entirely and we could see nothing but the poor devil's head. A yawl boat from a vessel got there first and picked him up, and, much to my surprise, for I thought he was gone. His boat, being heavily ballasted, probably went to the bottom. Whiskey has got on board somehow although the men were searched whenever they came from shore; several of them were put in double irons. Three men deserted this morning before daylight. I forgot to say that we have a passenger, Mrs. Kinkead of Sitka and her maid."

Mrs. Kinkead was the wife of John H. Kinkead who on July 23, 1867, had been appointed Postmaster at Sitka. He had arrived in Sitka aboard the *John L. Stephens* on October 9 but had returned south on the same ship. He arrived back in Sitka in mid-January, 1868, and opened the post office at that time. He also established a mercantile business and was appointed post sutler by the Army. The Kinkeads left Sitka in May 1871 and returned to Nevada where he was subsequently elected governor of the state. He returned to Sitka in 1884 as the first governor of the newly created District of Alaska.

Another passenger had been expected to go north on the *Saginaw* and perhaps to sign on as pilot in Alaska waters. He was Mikhail Kadin and had come south from Victoria in the *Saginaw*. Kadin was born on Atka Island, probably in 1830, and had been educated in St. Petersburg and was a cartographer and draftsman as well as a mariner. He was employed by the Russian-American Company with the rank of captain, charted some of the waters of western Alaska and drafted the charts for Tebenkov's *Atlas of the Northwest Coast of America*. In 1865 he became a pilot on one of the vessels chartered by the Western Union Telegraph Expedition and after the transfer, had served as pilot in United States vessels. In San Francisco while waiting for the *Saginaw* to sail he fell into a deep excavation at a construction site one evening and suffered a badly broken leg. He was in a hospital when the vessel sailed. Complications set in, he refused amputation of the leg and died on December 8.[8]

NOTES

1. Captain J. M. Frailey to Admiral T. T. Craven, aboard *Saranac* at Mare Island Navy Yard, October 21, 1868, U.S. Navy, U.S.S. *Saginaw* Collection, Folder "Letters Received and Forwarded," p. 61 (copy also available in typescript); Archives, Alaska and Polar Regions Department, Elmer E. Rasmuson Library, University of Alaska Fairbanks.

2. The *Alaska Herald* (San Francisco) 1(20):2 (Nov. 1, 1868).

3. Letter, Beardslee to R. W. Thompson, Secretary of the Navy, from Sitka, September 1, 1880. In "Affairs in Alaska" by Commander Beardslee, Senate Ex. Doc. 71, 47th Congress, 1st Session, v. 4.

4. The Schroeder quotation is from Seaton Schroeder, *A Half Century of Naval Service* (New York

and London: D. Appleton, 1922), p. 15. The biographical information is developed from *The Records of Living Officers of the U.S. Navy and Marine Corps* by Lewis R. Hamersly (3rd. ed., Philadelphia: J. B. Lippincott, 1878) and Dumas Malone, ed., *Dictionary of American Biography*, 21 vols. (New York: C. Scribner's Sons, 1933), vol. 12.

5. Meade to Commodore James Allen, commandant, Mare Island Navy Yard, November 21, 1868, in R. W. Meade Letterbook, p. 1. The Letterbook, hereafter cited as "Meade Letterbook," is owned by the New York Historical Society.

6. Meade to Commodore James Allen, Meade Letterbook, pp. 6-7.

7. Muster roll of USS *Saginaw*, January 1, 1869. Records of the Bureau of Naval Personnel, Record Group 24; on microfilm at Alaska Historical Library, Juneau, Ar 40, roll.

8. Richard A. Pierce, *Russian America: A Biographical Dictionary* (Kingston, Ontario, and Fairbanks, Alaska: The Limestone Press, 1990), pp. 209-210.

V

BACK TO SITKA

At 10 o'clock in the morning on Tuesday, December 1, 1868, the *Saginaw* again headed out through the Golden Gate, en route back to Alaska. There was a heavy swell on the bar but no breakers and the vessel was soon in the open ocean and heading up the coast.

Meigs: "Dec. 1, Tuesday. We left San Francisco at about 10½ A.M., battened the forward hatches but to no purpose, for we crossed the bar without shipping a single sea. Dick got news of his promotion [to full Commander] in the morning paper. As bad luck will have it, I am seasick, but there are several more on board in the same predicament. I think we are rather excusable, though, for it is as rough as the d----l."

The *Saginaw*'s officers for her second Alaska cruise, in addition to Commander Meade, were:

Master A. H. Vail, executive officer
Midshipmen E. W. Bridge, William Little, J. E. Pillsbury and Seaton Schroeder
Acting Surgeon W. H. Whidon
Acting Paymaster C. H. Lockwood
First Assistant Engineer A. H. Fisher
Second Assistant Engineer F. W. Townrow
Third Assistant Engineer Frederick Schober.
Fourth Assistant Engineer James Godfrey
Captain's Clerk P. Meigs

Among the officers only Vail, Whidon and Lockwood had been aboard on the previous Alaska cruise.

There were 54 in the enlisted crew, of whom 17 were rated as petty officers, 6 as seamen, 7 as ordinary seamen, 10 as landsmen, 8 as firemen and 6 as coal heavers.

The *Saginaw* had a rough trip up the coast and anchored in Victoria Harbor at 2:05 A.M. on December 7.

Meigs: "Dec. 2, Wed. I went on deck this morning and found we were driving along before a howling S.E. rainstorm, under our foresail, foretopsail and jib, but about noon, the wind changed very suddenly to N.W. causing us to take all our sails in. About 3 P.M. passed a barque, supposed to be the 'Delaware' from Sitka. Heavy sea.

"Dec. 3, Thurs. Head wind, heavy sea, rolling guards under about every other sea. At noon passed a schooner going south under double-reefed mainsail.

"Dec. 4, Fri. Head wind, heavy sea. Made land at about 3:40 P.M., some part of Oregon. I asked one of the Indians today what he would take for his sharks' tooth earrings and he said he gave ten blankets and a gun for them, so I concluded not to buy.

"Dec. 5, Sat. Land in sight all day. Made Mt. St. Helens at about 3½ P.M.; it is at the mouth of the Columbia River. There is quite a heavy sea on, and the spray flies clear over the pilot-house, which is well aft on the hurricane deck. I am in it now, writing, and find it difficult to keep my position although I am leaning on the log-desk. We are making about ten knots, and have been running all day under jib and fore and main trysails.

"Dec. 6, Sun. We had a pretty rough time last night; the officer of the deck told me that the spray broke almost up to our topmasts and flew in a perfect sheet, clear over the stern. I know I got very little sleep on account of the horrible rolling. When I went on deck this morning the view was perfectly *glorious*. Cape Flattery was in the distance and to the Northward and Eastward were immense mountains, about half of them covered with snow, and in the sunlight they looked like frosted silver; they are from 4-7,000 feet high. I never saw so many mountains together before in all my life. We passed

Tatouch Id. light (Cape Flattery) at 4 P.M. and are now steaming along in Juan de Fuca Strait about 40 miles from Victoria. Snow clad mountains can be seen in every direction. It has been blowing a howling North Easter for about two days and still continues. Sunday on shipboard seems to be no different from any other day."

The *Saginaw* picked up the harbor pilot, entered Victoria Harbor and dropped anchor at 2:05 A.M. on December 7. She spent six days there, during which the weather was rainy and drizzly. A schooner delivered 62 tons of coal to her and some other stores were loaded aboard. Peveril Meigs was able to keep busy during the stay:

Meigs: "Dec. 7, Mon. We struck bottom coming in here, (Victoria) last night, but although it shook us up a little, I believe there was no damage done. We *got* here about half past one o'clock last night, and on going on deck this morning, I wondered *how*, for we are in a little bit of a place just about room enough for us to swing at our anchor and the passage through which we came is only about 150 feet wide. I went on shore with Dick this morning intending to post a letter I wrote to mother last night but find there is no mail before Thursday, so I did not send it. It was a *perfect treat* to hear the dogs bark last night; it sounded like home. I won the pool this morning of about $5. -- in gold, for having guessed nearest to the time of letting go anchor here. I was introduced to the American consul this morning, and in the afternoon he brought his wife and daughter on board to call on Dick. His name is [Allen] Francis. I had an invitation to call from Miss. F. with whom I had quite a chat. Mrs. Kinkead made her appearance this morning for the first time since we left Frisco. She heard of the loss of the schooner 'Thomas Woodward' today, on its way to Sitka. She had all her household furniture on board; nothing was saved."

The *Thomas Woodward* was bound from San Francisco for Fort Wrangell and Sitka with military stores and supplies, civilian cargo and passengers. She was wrecked on November 25, 1868, at Cape Mudge, just south of Seymour Narrows in British Columbia. The vessel was a total loss but the passengers and some of the cargo were saved and were carried to their destinations by the Hudson's Bay Company steamer *Otter*. Whether Mrs. Kinkead's household goods were lost or saved was not reported.[1]

Meigs: "Dec. 8, Tues. Sent a letter to mother; also one to Hal. Meigs.

"Dec. 9, Wed. Went ashore with Mrs. Kinkead and did some shopping.

"Dec. 10, Thurs. Took a long walk to Beacon Hill where I had a splendid view. I was quite amused to see some Indians paddling around in their canoes shooting ducks and spearing fish. I sat on the rocks a long time (the surf breaking all around me), thinking of home and good friends. The place reminded me of Groton.

"Dec. 11, Fri. I forgot to say that 'His Excellency,' Gov. [Frederick] Seymour came on board yesterday with his secretary and took a look at the 'Saginaw,' remarking to Dick that she did not look much like a man-of-war, then, seeing that Dick didn't relish his sneer, qualified it by saying that he didn't see any pistols or boarding pikes around. He gave all the officers an invitation to lunch with him today, so five of us concluded to go; Dick sent a regret, *fortunately*. The Governor said he would send his carriage for us. We went ashore, jumped into the carriage and in fifteen or twenty minutes found ourselves at his house. He was occupied by business, so his wife received us about as cordially as an icicle. After about an hour's stupid conversation the Gov'r came in and we were ushered into the dining-room, where we found an ordinary home dinner set for us. Altogether there were 15 or 20 of us at the table, principally Englishmen; there were only three ladies, (*all* ugly.) The servants could not wait on us properly, so *I*, for one, nearly starved. The Gov'r and his Sec'y got up several times, went around the table several times helping themselves and back to their seats again to *devour* what they had been skirmishing for. After lunch we all went into the billiard-room where the *HOST* allowed a nasty subscription list to be presented to us. The Englishmen all put down ten or fifteen dollars apiece (gold), so of *course we* could not put anything very small so we put $25. -- and got no thanks. I think, by the way, the subject of 'the orphans' was introduced, that we were only invited there to be *dunned.* I felt ashamed for them. To cap the climax when we were ready to go we went to the door, accompanied by the Secretary, and looked around for the carriage in which we, (poor gulls), expected to ride home, but seeing the Sec'y bowing and backing into the house, we came to the sad and humiliating conclusion that they had got all they wanted out of us and now we could get home as best we could. So we started off with our pants turned up through the mud and mizzling rain back to the ship. Having had rain for four days past, and having on our thin boots, you can imagine how we enjoyed it. The distance we had to walk was over a mile. The English are a 'GREAT & MAGNANIMOUS PEOPLE' but you will never catch this 'chile' in one of their HOSPITABLE houses again. 'No, no! Not for Joe.' They are a DARN BLARSTED DIRTY SET OF BLARSTED ASSES.

"Dec. 12, Sat. Went ashore and played a couple of games of billiards with Mr. Pillsbury. We commenced coaling this morning.

"Dec. 13, Sun. Finished coaling about ten this morning. The hands were *obliged* to work for we were to have got under way today, but we will not start before tomorrow. I had to walk out to the Governor's this afternoon to return some charts he had sent to Dick to examine. Much to my satisfaction there was a sentry at the gate, so I was not obliged to set foot within his detestable house.

"Dec. 14, Mon. Got underway about 7½ A.M. Ran through Haro Strait, crossed Swanson Channel and went through Active Pass into the Strait of Georgia. Just before we entered the Pass, we were all wondering how we were to get out, for, directly in front of us was a large mountain and we ran until I thought we would run ashore, when the Pilot shouted, 'Hard a Port!' and we turned a beautiful point, starting up about a thousand wild ducks. The Pass was alive with them; they were black with a large white spot on each wing. In some places the water fairly *boiled* there were so many jumping up.

"I had a long talk with one of the sailors today; his name is Perry, he lives in Vermont and walked all the way from there to this country. He is a regular hunter and has his old Kentucky rifle on board. He told me of some scrapes he had in the woods with bears, particularly of one he shot on the Columbia River. He wants me to go hunting with him at Sitka, he says we will have to travel on snow-shoes and camp out under fir trees, but that suits me to a *dot*, so if Dick don't object I intend to go. This Perry is a first rate man. He seems to be about 45 years old, converses very well, uses very good language, and it puzzles me to know why he turned a hunter."

Alfred C. Perry was actually 35 years old, according to the ship's muster roll for January 1, 1869. He was born in New York State, was rated an ordinary seaman and had enlisted at Esquimault, the naval base near Victoria, on April 25, 1868, when the *Saginaw* was there under Commander Mitchell. His enlistment was for one year.

Meigs: "Dec. 15, Tues. We got nearly to Texada I'd last night, when it got so thick and blew so from the S.E., that we were obliged to lie to, all night, with quite a heavy sea running. Resumed our course again this morning. Strong S.W. wind so we have everything set that will draw and are making about ten knots per hour. At 10 A.M. took in the jibs and trysails. At twelve, being near Cape Mudge, and having a narrow passage to go through, we took in the topsail. We have had beautiful snow- capped mountains in sight all day, and the sun is shining quite brightly, something strange for this place.

"Dec 16, Wed. We anchored last night in Menzies Bay, a most beautiful little place, and as it was not quite dark, the pilot [Robert Hicks], Mr. Bridge and I went after some ducks, but although they were as thick as hops and were flying in immense flocks, we were unsuccessful. I only got one shot and that was a long, flying one and I missed. They got a few shots but their guns snapped. Got underway about 7 A.M. and ran with the tide through Seymour Narrows. The tide runs about 9 knots an hour here, and it is 1,000 feet deep in many places. The scenery here is just like the most beautiful parts of the Hudson; we go winding in and out among immense mountains, *dense* with foliage. The only drawback is that it rains nearly all the time. At noon we passed some *Extra* large mountains capped with snow and all along their sides were little rivulets, looking like silver threads. It is something more grand and beautiful than anything I have ever seen; beats the Hudson all to pieces. I got a little spooney this morning and read Enoch Arden. *Dear Old Fellow!* Mrs. Kinkead admired Carrie Cook's jockey hat pincushion very much. 9 P.M. We are now lying peacefully at anchor in Alert Bay with an Indian village in full view across the Strait. The pattering of the rain on deck will put 'dis Chile' to sleep.

"Dec. 17, Thur. Got underway about 4 A.M. About 10 A.M. passed the wreck of the 'Swanee'."

The 1,030-ton iron paddle steamer USS *Suwanee*, 12 guns, in command of Captain Richard Law, struck an unknown rock in Shadwell Passage, B.C., on July 9, 1968, while bound for Sitka and became a total loss. Her crew was rescued by HMS *Sparrowhawk* and taken to Victoria. The rock now appears on the charts as Suwanee Rock.

The *Saginaw*'s log reported on December 17: "At 10 A.M. passed wreck of the *Suwanee.* Stack still standing and paddle wheels and boilers apparently in good condition."

Meigs: Dec. 17, continued: "Crossed Queen Charlotte Sound in about four hours. 3 P.M., passed quite a large waterfall. Anchored in Bella Bella Harbor a little after 8 P.M. Dick had some trouble with the pilot. [It may have been this 'trouble' that led Commander Meade to fire Pilot Hicks at Sitka.]

"Dec. 18, Fri. Were unable to get underway this morning on account of the fog. The Indians from Bella Bella came around the ship and traded smoked salmon, etc., for tobacco. I gave two of the best looking squaws some kid gloves, a bottle of cologne and water, and a sachet, with which they seemed much pleased. Fog cleared up and we got underway about quarter of one P.M.

Ran an hour, when fog set in again, and, after coming within about ten feet of a rock, we came to anchor in a beautiful little cove about ten miles from Bella Bella. Several of us went ashore after ducks but were unable to get any. Perry gave us a sample of his shooting; he discovered fresh deer tracks on the beach but we couldn't find the deer. I never saw such thick woods before in my life; the trees are almost all firs and in some places they have fallen three and four deep, causing one to keep crawling over and under them in the more tiresome manner."

According to the ship's log, the anchorage was Kynumpt Harbor, Seaforth Channel, which had been named for the chief of a local Indian tribe.

Meigs: "Dec. 19, Sat. Got underway before daylight; crossed Milbank Sound. We had the most beautiful scenery today that we have had yet. Some of the mountains, densely wooded, were almost perpendicular and we ran within 30 feet of them, so that if you looked up it seemed as though the trees were almost overhead. We passed several pretty waterfalls, and saw it snowing on the tops of the mountains.

"Dec. 20, Sun. We ran all last night and stopped at Fort Tongas, an American port. (Thank the Lord we are in the United States again.) I left a letter for mother. We only stopped about half an hour, but that was long enough to excite my sympathy for the poor devils sent up here in the midst of the mountains, with nothing but Indians around them. We brought them the first news of the election [of Ulysses S. Grant as President of the United States; the *Saginaw* also brought mail for the post]. Excepting some in a small boat which we passed yesterday, these are the first white folks we have seen since we left Victoria.

"Dec. 21, Mon. We had to stop about ½ mile from Fort Wrangel last night [at Point Highfield] but we ran around to the Fort about daylight, left the mails and went right on. Why these places should be called forts is more than I know, for there are only a few log houses, etc., a number of soldiers and a flagstaff to be seen, nothing at all in the way of a stockade or defense of any kind. Some Indians came alongside in their canoes, with their faces painted red and black making them look perfectly *fiendish.* In a narrow pass, just before entering Prince Frederick Sound, we saw thousands of wild geese and ducks innumerable. Tried the fishing but got no bites. Has been freezing all day."

The "narrow pass" mentioned by Meigs was Wrangell Narrows and the *Saginaw* had to anchor for an hour and three-quarters to wait for high tide before entering. She passed through the narrows without incident, then through Frederick Sound and up Chatham Strait to drop anchor in front of Kootznahoo village, which was frequently spelled "Koutsnow" in the ship's log. The log reported: "At 8 sent boat ashore to land the Indians. 8:05, beat to quarters and uncovered the guns." P. Meigs recorded the full story:

Meigs: "Dec. 22, Tues. We stopped at Koutsnow this morning to leave the three Indian hostages, held for Mr. Ponti, Capt. Mitchell's clerk, who was left here some months ago. As no canoes came off to us, about 8 A.M. we lowered the cutter and Mr. Bridge went ashore in her with the Indians in charge. About 200 yards from the ship, the cutter was met by canoes filled with Indians who paddled alongside of it quite quietly until suddenly one of them fired his rifle, and Mr. B., not happening to be looking in that direction, imagined that it was firing at our boat. At the instant the shot was fired, the Indians raised a yell and the canoes began paddling for the land as fast as they could. Mr. B., in order to see what was going on before he landed, ordered the men to rest on their oars, which order was no sooner obeyed than one of the three Indians in the cutter seized one of the men, pulled him down in the bottom of the boat and tried to take his oar away from him. Mr. B., thinking now that they really did mean mischief, drew a revolver that I had lent him (the men were all unarmed and as uneasy as could be, and ordered the Indian to let the man up, which he did; then he ordered the men to pull for the ship as fast as they could. As soon as the cutter turned, we thought the fiends had shot someone, so all hands were beat to quarters, the guns were cast loose, the magazines opened, and every preparation made to blow Koutsnow to the four winds. It was quite exciting. When the cutter turned, the canoes turned also, and gave chase, overhauling our men easily. When they got even with them I thought sure I was going to see our men slaughtered right under my nose, so I rushed down into the cabin, loaded my gun with heavy shot in hopes of getting a crack at the villains, but all our fuss amounted to nothing for when the boat reached the ship, nobody was hurt, and much to our surprise, the canoes coming alongside at the same time, we were made to understand that they were only rejoicing at the return of their chiefs. Sic transit gloria! We lost our anticipated fun. We met the St'r 'Otter' about 4 P.M. on her way to Victoria, but Mr. Kinkead, who was on her, recognizing his wife on the 'Saginaw', persuaded the Capt. of the 'Otter', for a consideration of four or five hundred dollars, to return to Sitka, where we arrived at 6 P.M."

As the *Saginaw* neared the western end of Peril Strait after delivering the three Indian hostages at Kootznahoo, the log had this entry: "At 3:30 P.M. sighted steamer *Otter*. Stopped engines and sent mail to her."

It is unclear whether this was mail the *Saginaw* brought north for the *Otter* or was mail to be carried south. The *Otter*, as related earlier, had brought north the passengers and the salvaged cargo from the wrecked schooner *Thomas Woodward*. The passengers and cargo had first been delivered to Fort Tongass and Fort Wrangell. From the latter port the *Otter* carried to Sitka the bad news that the post hospital had been destroyed by fire, with all of the medicines, stores and supplies that were stored in the building. General J. C. Davis, in command of the military district, chartered the *Otter* to carry necessary equipment and supplies to Fort Wrangell and was on that mission when she met the *Saginaw* in Peril Strait.

The *Otter* did turn back to Sitka but surely not because John Kinkead paid her four or five hundred dollars to take him back there. He could easily have transferred to the *Saginaw* on the small boat that carried the mail. Probably the *Saginaw*, which had been at Fort Wrangell only two days earlier, was carrying a request for some additional equipment, supplies or even personnel. At any rate, the *Otter* did go back to Sitka, stayed overnight and left again at 8:30 the following morning for Victoria via Fort Wrangell.

Meigs, December 22, continued: "[Arrived at Sitka at 6 P.M.] I was the first one ashore for Dick sent me ashore to the Russian Consul's [probably Prince Maksutov] with some official documents relating to the $11,000.-- in specie we brought from San Francisco. Sent a letter to Jim Pratt by the 'Otter'.

"Dec. 23, Wed. Went ashore with the specie and got the percentage, 2%, for Dick for carrying it. In the afternoon I went with Dick to Gen'l Davis' where we were introduced to his wife, and spent quite a pleasant afternoon. The 'Otter' left here this morning. The days are very short; the sun rises about 9 A.M. and sets about 3 P.M. I have been ashore several times and had a chance to see something of Sitka. The inhabitants are chiefly Indians, about half of them paint their faces with red and black paint, giving them a fiendish expression. There are some Russians here but I believe the majority have gone to their own country. The balance seems to consist of U.S. soldiers. The town has for a background immense mountains, covered almost to their bases with snow which looks perfectly beautiful in the sunshine. The houses are mostly built of logs and fitted in real Russian style, fire places built right in the room, also immense crooked brass knobs on the doors, looking queer to a stranger."

NOTE

1. Records of the U.S. Customs Service at the Alaska Historical Library, Juneau.

VI

THREE WEEKS AT SITKA

The weather at Sitka that Christmas season was mostly clear and mild. On the morning of December 23 there was frost with a low of 26 degrees, according to the *Saginaw*'s dry bulb thermometer, but in the afternoon it went up to 34 degrees. The crew was kept busy cleaning the ship that day and the next.

Meigs: "Dec. 24, Thur. Christmas Eve. The first time I have ever been away from home on this happy day. Oh how many pleasant thoughts are passing through my mind. It is half past four P.M. here, making it about 8½ P.M. at home, the difference in time being about four hours. I can imagine Katie and Louise running around the house trying to get a peek at the Christmas tree and eager for the parlor doors to open. The hasty 'tea' eaten with little appetite on account of the excitement, everybody's face looking smilingly mysterious, kind words from everyone, and I wonder if they ever think of the one so far away. Good night all! God bless you and grant to you and to one in her home a 'Merry Christmas'."

On Christmas Day the sky was clear, the temperature from 28 to 37 degrees. In the morning the crew scrubbed the main deck with sand, after which a liberty party went ashore at 11 o'clock. Peveril Meigs, who included in his diary so many details of the voyage, failed to include the Christmas dinner menu aboard ship or at the home where he and Commander Meade were the guests. In fact, he seldom mentioned food in his writings.

Meigs: "Dec. 25, Fri. Spent the morning on board, thinking of home. Was very much amused at a curious form of punishment among the Indians. Two boys got fighting and one of them got hurt and cried out lustily, whereupon the father rushed out and, instead of knocking the boy down, as I thought he would, he simply pulled the boy's blanket off, leaving him shivering in the cold. In the afternoon Dick and I took dinner with Major and Mrs. [C. O.] Wood and Mrs. Kinkead, and had a very pleasant evening. Major Wood commanded Ft. Lafayette when Ben Corlies [Corliss] was shut up there. [Corliss later became Meigs' brother-in-law.]

"Dec. 26, Sat. Went ashore in the morning and saw some trading going on with the Indians at Mr. Kinkead's store. They got martin skins for $2.-- and $2.50 apiece (gold). Red foxes for $1.50. Rained all day."

On this rainy Saturday Commander Meade wrote a letter to Admiral T. T. Craven, commanding the North Pacific Squadron and said, in part:

> At this place I paid off and discharged coast pilot Robert Hicks, the person employed by Cmdr. Mitchell for $150 per month. He is a good pilot and interpreter but has been spoiled for service in a man-of-war by being allowed too much latitude. In mid-journey he refused to take the vessel to Sitka and I was obliged to deal in a summary manner with him. I soon brought him to his bearings and from that time forward had no further trouble, but I would not recommend him for employment in our vessels.[1]

It seems probable that the firing took place as soon as the *Saginaw* reached Sitka and that Hicks left aboard the *Otter* the following morning. Our only clue here is the statement by Meigs at Bella Bella that "Dick had some trouble with the pilot." That may have been where, according to Meade's letter, "he refused to take the vessel to Sitka." Hicks was British. Meade was noted for his hot temper and like most Union officers he had little use for Britain which had sided with the Confederacy during the Civil War. One can surmise that the two men did not hit it off and that Hicks wanted to get off the ship at Bella Bella until Meade's "summary manner" persuaded him to continue to Sitka.

In his letter to Admiral Craven on the 26th, Meade also wrote:

> I have communicated with General Davis who informs me that everything is working well in the Department [Military Department of Alaska] and the Indians are well disposed. I find no instructions among my predecessor's papers and shall therefore act according to my judgment and the circumstances of the moment until I hear from you. I secured coal at Victoria for $10 per ton or $8.75 cheaper than the Hutchinson & Kohl contract for Nanaimo coal at Sitka, an exorbitant price. At Nanaimo I can procure it for $8 per ton delivered on board. I think it would be advisable to establish a coal station at this point and believe coal can be shipped from Mare Id. Calif. cheaper than you can contract for the Nanaimo coal with any of the parties doing business here.
>
> So far as my limited observation extends the civilians in this Department are all in collusion to bleed the Gov't to the fullest extent possible. If necessary I can charter a schooner and load her with coal at Nanaimo and tow her to this place. The cost would be about $13 per ton.[2]

Two days after he wrote that letter, Commander Meade got a chance to try the *Saginaw* as a towboat. On December 27 Collector of Customs Hiram Ketchum sent word to the ship that the brig *Shelikoff* was in distress at the entrance to Sitka Sound. Commander Meade took a look at wind and sea conditions and decided the brig was becalmed rather than in distress. By the next day, however, he had changed his mind, hired a local pilot and went out to pass the brig a towline. The vessel was brought safely to an anchorage in the harbor but the *Saginaw*'s log noted, "Parted the hawser twice."

The 213-ton *Shelikoff* had been one of the Russian-American Company's vessels and came under the American flag on May 20, 1868. On November 24, 1868, the *Shelikoff* sailed from Sitka for San Francisco, in command of Captain Alexis Kuropteff. She carried a mixed cargo that included furs and hides, 21 mill stones, 900 barrels of flour, old iron, copper, rifles, anchors, chains and three barrels of cranberries.

After leaving Sitka the brig ran into head winds and rough seas and lost enough of her sails that she was all but unmanageable. That was when she put back to Sitka, but even when in harbor with her anchor down, her troubles were not over. She lost her jibboom during a heavy gale on the night of January 19 when the Revenue Cutter *Wayanda* dragged anchor and collided with her. It was not until February 12, two months and a half after her first departure, that she resumed her voyage. One wonders about those cranberries.

Meigs: "Dec. 27, Sun. Dick was taken quite sick last night with cholera morbus and kept his bunk nearly all day. I made all my arrangements with Perry for going hunting tomorrow. Wrote a letter to mother, to be ready for the barque that will sail in the beginning of January.

"Dec. 28, Mon. I was prevented from starting on our hunting party today by an infernal brig that has been lying off the harbor for a couple of days. Dick refused to go after her at first, as he heard there was nothing the matter with her, but last night they sent a letter saying she was in distress, so of course we had to get up steam and towed her in. There was nothing the matter with her, they were only impatient to get in, so I suspect they will have to pay for the coal and pilot. Perry and I will start tomorrow morning if we can hire a canoe, and as Dick has been trying to scare me for several days by hinting about being frozen to death, scalped by Indians, killed by bears, upset in the canoe, and is sure he will never see me again, I feel almost as though something really *will* happen, so I here say goodbye to all my friends, relations, etc., wishing them a very happy New Year, even if I am not to enjoy the same! Now don't congratulate yourselves for you may be sure a bad penny like me will certainly come back to bother you.

"Dec. 29, Tues. Copied from small journal. 'Camp Comfort', near Sitka. Here we are at last. Perry and I sit by our campfire, and I am writing by its light, on my cartridge box. We have got an Indian with us and I can see him through the blaze looking in the most stoical manner into the fire. Perry and I have just settled the name of the camp. We left the ship at one P.M., which did not give us much time to get to the hunting grounds; so we stopped on this island after night overtook us. Perry is smoking the pipe of peace, the moon is just rising above the snow-clad peaks, the fire is blazing brightly (large logs), and altogether it is very romantic. Ham and hardtack for supper! Oh how Jim Pratt would enjoy this. Our boughs and blankets are spread so I will bid the world 'good-night' and the plash of the waves will soon lull me to sleep. I *think* the Indian is safe, but I will sleep with my rifle and revolver close alongside of me in case of accident.

"Dec. 30, Wed. I did not sleep very well last night, for it seemed so strange for me to be sleeping in the open air, with nothing but the trees and the heavens for a covering, and besides this it was rather cold. We left 'Camp Comfort' early this morning and directed our course to the low land near Mt. Edgecomb but on our way the Indian used a little too much muscle and broke his paddle, so we were obliged to stop and make a new one, but in spite of all the difficulties we arrived at our permanent camp about noon, started our fire, cooked some slices of ham on sticks, made some tea, and in very short time exit ham and tea. Perry and I then took a stroll through the forest in search of deer, but returned about dark, unsuccessful. The beauty of the forest fully repaid us for our walk, the ground is an entire network of fallen trees covered with beautiful moss, no briars of any account to impede our progress, and not a very thick undergrowth. The frost looks like snow, with the exception that it is in larger crystals, and it covers the moss about half an inch deep, so that every step you take makes a crisp, crushing sound which is very refreshing to hear. Scattered very thickly in the moss are ferns and hundreds of different little plants still more beautiful, all perfectly green, and covered partially with the frost crystals, making the ground so perfectly lovely that it seemed almost wicked to mar its beauty with our foot-prints, and to add still more to the effect, every tree is a X'mas tree already draped with vines and hanging moss.

"Dec. 31, Thurs. 2½ P.M. It has been a lovely day, the sun still shining brightly, but is very nearly down. It rises about 9 A.M. and sets about 3 P.M. this time of year, thus making the nights very long. Perry went hunting alone this morning and the Siwash (Indian) man and I went together. We started as soon as it was quite light, about nine o'clock and after a long walk over hills and through valleys, following the different trails, returned to camp quite crestfallen, with one unfortunate duck that we shot just before entering camp. We found Perry busy cutting up a small deer that had been wounded by someone and, in jumping across a small brook, had broken its leg by falling on the ice and died. It is frozen solid and is perfectly fresh, probably having been shot within one or two days. As this is the first fresh meat we have had since we left the ship, we relish it immensely. Perry and I have just finished our dinner and now the Indian is 'sailing in' like a wolf. Three large pieces of the deer are still roasting on the ends of sticks stuck in the ground before the fire, and I can assure you the frizzling sound is delicious to hear. Our camp is beautifully situated.

(Sketch.)

"When we landed it was calm, but now, although there is no wind, the breakers are piling in about ten feet high, making reports like cannons. They come rushing in through a little channel marked 'A', which is only about 15 feet wide and filled with rocks, in a beautiful sheet of pure white foam. They strike on the rock marked 'B', which is about 20 feet high, some flying away up in the air as spray and the rest pouring over the side towards us in a perfect cataract. It is a little cold sleeping nights, but we keep up a good fire and wrap up well in our blankets, thus managing to stand it pretty well. The coldest operation is washing our faces and hands in the morning, as we have to break the ice to get at the chuck (water) and when we *do* get it, it is hi-as cool (very cold). Tea and roast venison for supper. Good Bye, Old Year, Good Bye!

"Jan. 1, Fri. 'Happy New Year, Mr. Meigs!' was the first thing that rang in my ears on waking this morning. The salutation came from poor old Perry and Oh how many happy thoughts crowd upon my mind when I think of the jolly times going on at Staten Island; of Katie and Louise and everybody running through our *dear* old home shouting 'Happy New Year to all,' while I, shut out from the world in a dense, damp Russian American forest, send up this same wish for all at home and all my friends, with all the heartiness I am capable of. On getting up I found the ground covered about an inch deep with snow and the outside of my blanket as though it was covered with diamonds. Broke the ice in the brook and had a *nice cool* wash. I took breakfast and then started out for a stroll along the beach hoping to get some ducks, but before I got far I found I could not walk without my knee hurting me owing to a fall I had on the rocks while exploring the island in front of our camp. So I returned and as Perry did not want to go into the brush until the snow had blown off, we staid near camp all day together. Got a line. . . The Siwash was in the woods all day but found no 'mowitch' (deer). Something has depressed me for two days. I can't imagine what it is unless it is the constant . . . of the surf, night and day, which gives one a feeling of . . ., such as a murder-story inspires. I long to see -------. We had venison stew for dinner. The Indian ate the brains and skin from the deer's head. We call this 'New Year Camp.' I was lazy today and *made no calls* (except for meals).

"Jan. 2, Sat. It began to snow last night just as we turned in and kept on doing so almost all night; today also it has been snowing at intervals. Had duck stew for breakfast and found it *first rate*, not fishy a bit. We all had to keep near camp today on account of the snow. Perry ventured out in the afternoon and saw a fine doe, but the animal was too sharp for him and did not let him get a shot, so, it being near dark, he came back, intending to follow the trail tomorrow morning.

"Jan. 3, Sun. Rained like the mischief last night and obliterated the trail, so we gave up the chase, and as we were all rather wet and there seemed no hope of pleasant weather, concluded to start for the 'Saginaw.' So after some difficulty, we got the canoe in the water in the lee of some rocks, and, after shooting some ducks, made for the islands. We had about five miles of open ocean to cross, and as ill luck would have it, a violent hail and rain squall came up, catching us about midway, so we squared away for the nearest land and, after considerable tossing, reached a little bay in safety. As soon as the squall let up a little, we managed to get around a rocky point and found ourselves in the very same place where we made the paddle, so we found a snug little place under some tree, built a fire, got something to eat and turned in for the night after Perry's reading about a dozen chapters in the Bible, in the most sing-song manner, causing the Siwash much merriment. About three o'clock in the morning, I woke and heard a slight rustling about two feet from my head. As it was still snowing hard, I thought it was the grass settling under the weight, so I was closing my eyes again, but happening to move my head a little, I heard something stirring, very distinctly, so I seized my revolver and sat up just in time to see a coyote or some such beast about the size of a dog, scamper off in a tremendous hurry, getting beyond the light of the fire before I could shoot. The villain had been looking for our eatables.

"Jan. 4, Mon. Started again at daylight for the ship, succeeded in getting 3 or 4 miles when we were caught by a sharp squall, accompanied with snow, hail and rain. The canoe being very crank, we came with an ace of being upset, but after some effort we got behind a point of land, went ashore, built a fire and tried in vain to dry ourselves. Two Indians came into our camp, toasted their feet awhile, loaded their guns and disappeared in the woods; these are the first we have seen since we left Sitka. In the afternoon we managed to paddle about half a mile further, and then had to camp again for the night, (blowing like the D----l!). Everything but my blanket sopping wet. After many futile attempts, we got a fire going, cooked some supper, turned in for the night. And *I*, strange to say, had a pleasant dream of home.

"Jan. 5, Tues. Pleasant morning, for a wonder. Got under way about daylight and after shooting awhile at the poor ducks, got to the ship safely about 11½ A.M." [Continued later.]

On January 2, 1869, Commander Meade wrote to Admiral T. T. Craven:

> Although the value of this territory, in my judgment, has been very much over-rated, yet our acquisition of it will soon lead to a considerable development

of its resources and to that end the emigration of our citizens to these shores must hereafter be permanently watched over by a military and naval force.

I therefore suggest that Japonski I'd opposite the town of Sitka and near which men-of-war moor, offers a very secure site for a store house and coal shed and from which a wharf is already constructed.

I respectfully suggest that a supply of coal and naval stores be shipped to this place as soon as possible and an officer charged to take care of them here when landed. In this way the vessels of the squadron may be replenished without being at the mercy of the parties doing business here, who all combine to extract from the government all they can.

Sitka is a central point from which all exploring parties must start. If six large mooring buoys can be laid down near the island, a very fair naval station is, at once, established, for although the gales of autumn and winter are very violent, yet the sea is always smooth and good holding facilities the only thing needful. A vessel cannot well use her own ground tackle since the bottom is shaley and a vessel rides solely by the weight of her anchor. Buoys well put down will make this place secure in all weather.

There is no coal here now and none to be procured. I have but 30 tons. Wood is cheap and until I hear from you I can cruise very economically by cutting it or having the Indians do so.

After the quarterly returns are sent off I shall visit Kootznahoo and ascertain how much of the coal taken out by Mitchell remains. I should not care to use it unless driven by necessity to do so, since the experiment last summer proved a costly one to the government, several thousand dollars being needed to repair damages to the boilers and stack.

It is to be hoped the Coast Survey vessels may get to work this spring. Wrangell Straits, Revilla-Gigedo Channel, Kootznahoo Bay, Peril Strait and Sitka Bay should be the first places examined.[3]

Ship's log, Friday, January 1: "At 6:15 P.M. crew called to general quarters. Loaded pivot gun with shell and howitzers with shrapnel. Fired a shrapnel to the left of town. Sounded retreat at 8 P.M. but the starboard watch remained by the guns. 3rd cutter went out on picket duty."

Log, Saturday, January 2: "Battery cast loose and watch at quarters. 3rd cutter on picket duty. Got out a spring so the guns would bear on the Indian village."

Log, Tuesday, January 5: "Sent 3rd cutter and gig after a canoe. They returned when it landed."

Commander Meade to Admiral T. T. Craven, from Sitka January 7, 1869:

> Since my last letter I have the following to report. On New Years night a difficulty took place on shore between the guard and some Chilkat Indians headed by their chief. One soldier and two Indians were kept dangerously wounded. Gen'l Davis requested me to co-operate with the Army by preventing the escape during the night of the Chilkat chief. I acceded to his wish and sent an armed boat in charge of Mdm. J. E. Pillsbury to picket the stream to the westward of the Indian village. The cutter drove back some six canoes, being obliged to fire a volley at one. The next day the Chilkat chief was captured and is now in the guard house. A good deal of bad feeling between the Indians and the military has been engendered by the occurrence but I think there will be no further difficulty unless Gen'l Davis releases the Chilkat chief when trouble with that tribe develops, as I look for.[4]

The Meigs diary has a somewhat different version of the events. His entry for January 5, continued: "We were hailed [when returning to the ship] in a very angry and excited manner by some Indians on an island and, thinking their canoe had gone adrift and that they wanted to cross to Sitka, we made for them, but on nearing the shore I saw they had their rifles and were very much excited, so we concluded to have nothing to do with them. When we got near the ship, we were met by Mr. Pillsbury in the dingy, who told us there had been trouble with the Indians and that two of them and one soldier had been killed and two or three Indians wounded. It seems that the officer of the guard, on shore, gave an order to the sentry on the wharf, not to allow any canoes to pass during the night as a soldier had been killed in a melee with the Chilcats and the Chilcat 'Hyas Tyee' had been taken prisoner, and he had heard an attempt was to be made in the night by the Indians to liberate him. This order was to be in force during the night only, but the sentinel had no order to that effect, so he passed it to the relief, and in the morning a canoe with six or seven Indians attempted to pass, and when they only paddled faster when hailed by the sentinel, he fired into them four times, killing one and wounding one. When Dick saw the row, he supposed the trial had been made to liberate the chief, so having already had notice that the Indians meant mischief, he sent two boats in chase. The canoe would not stop, so they fired several shots at it, some of them striking it, but whether wounding any of the Indians or not we don't know. Some more canoes filled with Indians started from the village, Dick thought to help those being chased, so he had a howitzer loaded with canister, trained at them, and, after firing a few shots with a rifle himself at them, he put a bullet into one canoe and caused them to go back. The Indians that were chased by our boats ran their canoe into the surf where our men could not follow, landed on the island, and were the same that hailed Perry and me coming in. They evidently took us for Indians, and I don't blame them, for *I* was wrapped in a red blanket, making me look very like one, but if we had gone ashore and they had seen that we belonged to the ship, I think it likely that both of us might have lost our 'har'.

"Jan. 6, Wed. Nothing of any interest took place today. I wrote a postscript to Mother's letter, telling her of my hunting trip. We have been expecting the Revenue Cutter to arrive (the 'Wayanda') from San Francisco, with mails from home. She came in this afternoon but nary mail. We are very much disappointed for there may not be another arrival for one or two months."

On her way to Sitka the *Wayanda*, Captain J. W. White, on December 30 struck a rock, today known as California Rock, in Tongass Narrows. A Board of Survey was convened at Sitka and found that her false keel was turned up and badly torn and her main keel was splintered from the bow to the middle of the fore-chains, and that some of her copper was gone. "It is imperative that she be hauled out in dry dock and repaired as early as possible," the board reported on January 15.[5]

The *Wayanda*, which had been outfitted for a summer of cruising in Alaska waters, unloaded her spare subsistence stores at Sitka on January 22 and sailed south. On a later voyage she touched on a reef in Sergius Narrows north of Sitka. It is now known as Wayanda Ledge.

Meigs: "Jan. 6, Thurs. Wrote to Will Hall. Gen'l Davis and Capt. [George H. A.] Dempfel [Dimpfel] came on board during the day.

"Jan. 7, Fri. Confined to the cabin all day by the rain. The bark by which we intend to send our letters has made no preparations for starting. It has been blowing quite a gale for two or three days and the sailors on the bark being Russians, are probably afraid to start.

"Jan. 8, Sat. I wrote to Carrie Cook last night, and just before I wrote our steward came on board as tight as a brick and was put in irons for the night. I wish him pleasant dreams. It is nothing new for him to get drunk, but heretofore, Dick has been very lenient with him and this is the first time he has had him in irons."

Drunkenness was a frequent cause of disciplinary action as were overstaying leave and going ashore without leave. The captain's steward, Francisco Chavers, was in irons at least twice more during the voyage. In an attempt to curb the drunkenness, Commander Meade wrote to General Davis on January 13:

> I request that whenever the *Saginaw* is at Sitka that liquor dealers be prohibited from selling her crew any liquor.[6]

Meigs: "Jan. 10, Sun. Dick went to church this morning and while he was ashore the bark 'Menshikoff' sailed and I was sent in the gig to take our mail on board, which I did with much pleasure for I am tired of seeing it in the cabin."

The *Menshikoff*, 223 tons, was a former Russian-American Company vessel and had come under the American flag on January 25, 1868. On this voyage she was either owned or chartered by Hutchinson, Kohl & Co. and was in command of Captain W. W. Pavlov. She carried 13 passengers, including Prince Dimitri Maksutof, the former Russian-American Company chief manager, who was leaving Alaska for good.

The Russian warehouses at Sitka were being emptied of the vast store of merchandise they had held at the time of the transfer. The *Menshikoff*'s cargo, consigned to Hutchinson, Kohl, included 11 kegs of nails, 72 pieces of machinery, 18 tons of salt, a ton and a half of copper, two and a half tons of old iron, 350 pounds of iron kettles, and several hundred barrels, boxes, bales, cases and packages listed as "merchandise," the whole valued at $24,610.[7]

Meigs: "Jan. 11, Mon. The bark did not get out yesterday, but left last night, so our letters are on their way home. The steward came on board again today *undeniably* drunk; he was put in double irons, ducked with salt water and left for the night to his pleasant meditations.

"Jan. 12, Tues. I forgot to say that 'Jake,' a Koutsnow Indian, one of the three we had on the ship coming from San Francisco, came on Sunday in his canoe, with his 'klootchman' (woman), and several other Indians, to Sitka, stopping at the ship to see how we all were. He was gotten up in his marine uniform and looked quite fine. The officers gave him lots of tobacco and he went ashore quite pleased, especially when some one said, 'Boston man mica tillicum!' (Boston man is your friend.) He also came on board yesterday to trade skins but he had no very fine ones and none would trade. We had a grand scuffle tonight in the steerage; lots of fun! No heads broken but mine and that makes little difference for it was cracked before."

Notes

1. Meade Letterbook, pp. 10-11.
2. Meade Letterbook, pp. 9-12.
3. Meade Letterbook, pp. 23-26.
4. Meade letterbook, pp. 29-30.
5. Report from the Board to Collector Hiram Ketchum, U.S. Customs Records, Alaska Historical Library, Juneau.
6. Meade Letterbook, pp. 32-33.
7. Manifest of the *Menshikoff*, U.S. Customs Records, Alaska Historical Library, Juneau.

VII

KOOTZNAHOO COAL

Two sea-going branches of the United States government were involved during Alaska's early years under the American flag — the U.S. Revenue Marine Service and the U.S. Navy. Each service experimented with sending all-sail vessels to Southeastern Alaska and each decided that only steamers could adequately serve in the many protected waterways of that area.

Steamers required an assured and reliable source of fuel, either wood or coal, for their furnaces, with coal much preferred. The Russian-American Company had maintained a small coal depot on Japonski Island at Sitka to supply its steamers, bringing coal there from a mine at Port Graham, Cook Inlet. That mine did not operate after the transfer and the Americans shipped coal from British Columbia or other points to Sitka. That had some drawbacks, one of which was the cost.

Whether Lieut.-Commander John G. Mitchell's instructions, when he took the USS *Saginaw* to Southeastern Alaska in the spring of 1868 included a search for local coal sources is not known, but when he learned of coal deposits he investigated them. His first such venture was on Kupreanof Island at the place he named Hamilton Bay, as related in Chapter 3. About three tons of coal was mined there, but the seam was small and Commander Mitchell did not return to that site.

The next investigation was at Kootznahoo Inlet which penetrates deeply into the western side of Admiralty Island at the present day village of Angoon. The inlet features some fast tides, known as "skookum chucks" in the Chinook Jargon.

Commander Mitchell wrote to Admiral T. T. Craven an account of his first visit to Kootznahoo Inlet:

> From Saginaw Bay we sailed on the 4th of July for Katznoo and finding the anchorage bad in front of the village, ran in behind the little island [Killisnoo Island] showing on the chart, anchoring in 9 fms water; this a very snug anchorage. We had come up to this point to look at and try some coal said to exist and of which an Indian had brought some fine specimens.
>
> On the morning of the 5th I took the gig and started to go to look for it, and also to see whether there was water enough for the vessel, which there was some dispute about.
>
> On entering you go for about a mile, until you come to the first rapids where the water runs, on a good Spring tide, about 9 or 10 knots per hour. Entering the rapids, keeping the large rock close to the starboard hand, you run half way between the starboard shore and a large rock on the port shore, turning sharp around to port, to avoid the danger of the higher [?] channel. The turn is about 28 points of the compass. About 5 miles above is another rapid, very narrow but tolerably straight, and current as swift if not swifter than the other, but not as dangerous.
>
> Some five miles further on we found the coal. After looking at the thing, carefully, I concluded to try the vessel at it, and the next day at 1 P.M. we started, going with the boat ahead to sound, and give warning of danger in case we discovered anything not seen the day previous.
>
> We had to make her get out of our way, though, in both rapids, for we had to steam all she would go to keep steerage way in such a current, it was with us all the way, and fortunately too as we touched on a rock above and near the coal. The vessel was going about 1½ knots at the time, the bell having just been rung 'Ahead Slow' and the steam down to six pounds. As soon as the steam was up again, with a kedge out on the starboard quarter and the line to the shaft, she came off very easily. The cast before touching showed (13) thirteen fathoms. We had the boat ahead and they did not have less than 10 fms. except once (4) four. After getting off anchored in 9 fms. soft bottom.

> I staid at the anchorage some two days and took out 18 tons coal very pretty. I send you a piece as a sample. The slab originally weighed half a ton, but in blasting near it, it broke into several pieces. This is an outside piece, and is not so good as it gets to be when you get farther into the hill.
>
> On the morning of the 9th July, by steam log, I find that at 2:45 A.M., started fires in (4) four furnaces, and at 3:30 A.M. steam formed. This was in 45 minutes, or 10 minutes sooner than with the best of our Navarins coal, and 13 minutes quicker than the Hamilton Bay coal.
>
> After 12 hours steaming it was quite up to my expectations, showing only 20 per cent of ashes and dirt. Since then I have used it under only one boiler, and in smooth water making (9) knots easily; could have more but am afraid to raise the pressure on the boilers.
>
> I am going to get out a couple of hundred tons, and am quite certain it can be done at an expense of less than (7) Dolls in Greenbacks. You need not ship any more up here. I will supply myself.[1]

According to the ship's log they got 30 bags of coal aboard on July 7 and 98 on the 8th for a total of 128. That doesn't seem to add up to the 18 tons reported by Commander Mitchell in his letter to Admiral Craven. The Navy measured its coal in long tons, 2,240 pounds, and 18 tons would be 40,320 pounds. Coal sacks in common use held 100 pounds, but 128 bags would have to hold 315 pounds apiece to add up to 18 tons.

From Kootznahoo the *Saginaw* went to Sitka on July 9 and while there received on board 405 feet of lumber (39 boards), 200 pounds of blasting powder, five picks, six shovels and a sledge hammer. From Sitka the ship went south as far as Port Simpson in British Columbia and did not get back to Kootznahoo until July 25.

When the *Saginaw* arrived off the entrance to the inlet on the 25th the current was too strong to buck and it was not until 5:02 P.M. that the anchor was dropped off the coal mine. The next day 22 Indians were hired as laborers and they, with some of the crew from the ship got out 21 tons 400 pounds of coal in four days and transported it to the ship in boats and canoes.

The ship then went on a cruise to the northward, up Lynn Canal, and returned to the coal mine on August 1. Mate John Ponte was put ashore to take charge of the Indian laborers and continue to get out coal. There had been some friction, aboard ship, between Ponte and the executive officer, Master C. C. Bunker and on July 5, according to the log, "John Ponte, mate, placed under arrest per Commanding Office for insolence to the executive officer." Two days later the log said, "Mate John Ponte released from arrest temporarily by order of Commander."

Was it part of Ponte's punishment to be sent ashore at Kootznahoo to boss 22 Indians described by Mitchell as "not particularly tame"?[2] Or was he so desperate to get off the *Saginaw* and away from Bunker that he volunteered for the duty? Whatever the answer, he did go ashore, with 39 boards with which to build himself a shelter and with a Sharps carbine for protection.

After putting Ponte ashore at Kootznahoo, the *Saginaw* went to Sitka where 38 tons of coal from British Columbia were taken aboard. That raises the question whether, in the light of Commander Mitchell's July 10th statement to Admiral Craven — "You need not ship any more [coal] up here. I will supply myself" — he was now having second thoughts about the quality if not the quantity of coal obtained at Kootznahoo.

If Commander Mitchell did have doubts, his actions did not show it. He took the ship back to Kootznahoo where 444 more bags of coal were loaded on August 6 and 7. And, according to the log on the 6th, "Placed three Indians in double irons for creating trouble on shore." No other indication of "trouble" appears in the log or in Commander Mitchell's correspondence. It may be that the three were demanding that the laborers be paid for their work. Commander Mitchell did not pay them and made no arrangements for paying them. It was fairly well understood, however, by Commander Meade when he took command of the *Saginaw*, that the Indians were hostages for the safety of John Ponte. There is little doubt that Commander Mitchell planned, after completion of repair work at Victoria, to return to Kootznahoo, pick up Ponte and release the Indians. It did not work out that way, as seen in Chapter 3.

The *Saginaw* steamed southward to Victoria and San Francisco and did not return to Kootznahoo until December 22 when, under Commander Meade, the ship stopped briefly and sent a boat ashore to land the three Indians seized in August. In the meanwhile John Ponte and the Indian laborers got out 51 tons of coal and he had the Indians take him to Sitka in their canoes. It is perhaps a little surprising that the Indians did not take a leaf from Commander Mitchell's book and hold Ponte hostage. But they took him to Sitka, not knowing whether they would ever see the *Saginaw* again, or be paid for their labors. Ponte hitched a ride to San Francisco aboard the Revenue Cutter *Wayanda* and briefly rejoined the *Saginaw* at Mare Island.

Commander Meade had already expressed his disapproval of Kootznahoo coal in letters to Admiral Craven and quoted in Chapter 3.[3] Nevertheless, he towed a lighter to Kootznahoo Inlet from Sitka in January 1869 to pick up the coal mined by the Indians under Ponte's direction. On February 1 he wrote to Admiral Craven:

> I took on board 51 tons of coal at Kootznahoo, paid the Indians and had 22 cords of hemlock cut. Using a combination of Kootznahoo coal and green wood we can steam at 8 knots at a cost of $32 per day. Had the coal been purchased at Sitka the cost would have been $206.25 per day.
>
> The coal mine at Kootznahoo is practically exhausted so far as our use is concerned. A shaft would have to be sunk if mining were to continue there.
>
> The debts to the Indians who mined the coal having been paid, friendly relations with the Kootznahoo tribe are restored. They had commenced to feel angry and dissatisfied at not being paid for their labor; very naturally, as they had heard nothing from any Government officer since last September.
>
> Rather than paying them in money, I caused the Paymaster to purchase at Sitka some [illegible] articles of clothing, calico and leaf tobacco which they took more readily than money which they don't understand or appreciate the value of.

The cost of the coal was:

Paid Andre (Indian) for superintending laborers	$15.56
Paid Indians for mining and delivering coal	60.00
Paid Indians for carrying Mr. Ponte to Sitka	23.00
Paid for tools contracted by Mitchell	31.25
Total	$129.81
Paid Indians for 22 cord wood at $1.50	$ 33.00

"They cut a cord of wood for 6 yards of calico and it doesn't matter whether it cost 12½ or 25 cents a yard. It is quantity, not quality, that interests them."[4]

After he hit on the idea of burning the Kootznahoo coal with green hemlock, Commander Meade not only picked up the coal that had been mined under the direction of John Ponte but himself put a crew ashore to mine some more.

On January 17 according to the ship's log, "Entered Kootznahoo Archipelago and anchored at 12 noon in Mitchell Bay." That was the first time the name appeared in the log. Commander Meade had named the bay for his former classmate. After putting ashore 79 coal bags to be filled, the *Saginaw* left the inlet and did not return there until February 18 when the anchor was dropped "off Davis Creek in Mitchell Bay." Commander Davis had honored General Jefferson C. Davis, USA, military commander at Sitka, by naming the feature for him.

A crew was sent ashore the following day with, according to the log, 7 picks, 13 shovels, 1 hammer, 3 drills and 1 grindstone for working the coal mine. Indians were hired both to help load the coal on the lighter that had been towed from Sitka in January, and to cut wood. The *Saginaw* remained in the bay until February 22. The Meigs diary had this report on the stay there:

"Feb. 17, Wed. Got underway at 7:30 A.M. and arrived at Koutsnow at 3:10 P.M. We were unable to go through the rapids on account of the tide, so we came to anchor. When ebb-tide made, we dragged and were obliged to get underway again. We ran around the point to the opposite side of the neck of land on which Koutsnow stands and let go anchor within a stone's throw of the village at 8:45 P.M.

"Feb. 18, Thurs. The Indians hoisted the American flag this morning. Got underway at 10:25 A.M.; ran in safety through both rapids and Mitchell's bay and anchored near the coal mine at 2:55 P.M. We went ashore and found three veins of coal. The country here seems to be full of it. Was ashore among the Siwashes all the afternoon.

"Feb. 19, Fri. Went ashore just after breakfast and staid until half past three, watching the men blast, walking on the beach, in the woods, and amusing myself by talking to the klootchman. Gathered some leaves, etc.

"Feb. 20, Sat. Nothing important took place today except that we found a large vein of coal.

"Feb. 21, Sun. This is in *reality* a *Sun*-day, something very unusual, although we have had three or four quite pleasant days in succession. We have succeeded in mining about 25 tons of coal since we have been here.

"Feb. 22, Mon. Washington's Birthday, or, as the Siwashes call it, 'Hyas Sunday'. Got underway at 10:05 A.M.; ran down to where the Indians had the wood cut; took on a large deckload and filled the lighter. Left Koots-na-hoo at 5:10 P.M. I had a little package to give to one of the little klootchman, and was quite disappointed at not seeing her before we left. Came to in Dead Man's Bay at 12:50 P.M." [This was Deadman Reach, named Deadman Bay by Commander Meade.]

Commander Meade had his final say on Kootznahoo coal in a letter to Admiral Craven from Sitka on February 26, 1869:

> In our recent cruise to the Kake country we were absent from Sitka 12 days, were under steam all the time and the expense for fuel was about $105 or not quite $9 per day. I have on board 20 tons of Kootznahoo coal and about 30 cords of hemlock wood.
>
> At Kootznahoo we discovered fresh fields of coal, one seam being 5 feet wide, how deep I cannot say as we

only worked it down 2 feet and it can only be worked at low water.

Kootznahoo Archipelago is located in a valley between two ranges of lofty mountains, and I am perfectly satisfied is a vast field of coal. As to its quality, I have already made my report.

I continue to think it unsuitable and dangerous on shipboard owing to being so highly charged with resinous material. We have had to exercise great care in its use and I do not think we should have been so successful had we not used green wood with it. Our grate bars are very old and were not replaced at Mare Island, consequently they are giving out.[5]

That was the end of the Navy's effort to mine coal in Kootznahoo Inlet. Coal was mined there off and on during the next 45 years or so by a number of individuals and companies and was marketed in Sitka and Juneau. It was not until 1914 that the Navy again attempted to utilize Alaska coal and then it was coal from the Matanuska Valley.

Notes

1. Lt.-Commander John G. Mitchell to Rear Admiral H. K. Thatcher, Sitka, July 10, 1868, U.S. Navy, U.S.S. *Saginaw* Collection, Folder "Letters Received and Forwarded," pp. 73-77 (copy also available in typescript); Archives, Alaska and Polar Regions Department, Elmer E. Rasmuson Library, University of Alaska Fairbanks).

2. Lt.-Commander John G. Mitchell to Rear Admiral Thomas T. Craven, Victoria, V.I., August 22, 1868, U.S. Navy, U.S.S. *Saginaw* Collection, Folder "Letters Received and Forwarded," pp. 65-67 (copy also available in typescript); Archives, Alaska and Polar Regions Department, Elmer E. Rasmuson Library, University of Alaska Fairbanks.

3. Dated at Mare Island Navy Yard on November 27, 1868, and at Sitka on December 26, 1868. Meade Letterbook pp. 4-5.

4. Meade Letterbook, pp. 34-39.

5. Meade Letterbook, p 60.

VIII

A CRUISE TO THE EASTWARD

The narrative of the *Saginaw*'s voyage is continued here from the end of Chapter 6. The ship's log noted on January 13: "Pilot James Keene came aboard. Up anchor at 11:45."

James W. Keen (the correct spelling of his name), like his predecessor aboard the *Saginaw*, was born in England but some 14 years later, in 1842. He began a four-year apprenticeship aboard a Hudson's Bay Company steamer in 1859 and came to the Pacific Coast in the ship that year. In 1869 he was probably less experienced than Hicks as a pilot, especially in Alaska waters. Young Meigs picked up bits of the Chinook jargon, much used by the Hudson's Bay Company, from both pilots, and it was undoubtedly with their help that he compiled a list of words and phrases from that lingua franca.

Keen continued as a pilot in both government and commercial vessels for many years and last renewed his license in 1927. Keene Island and Keene Channel at the juncture of Wrangell Narrows and Beecher Pass, were named for him, as was Keene Rock in Sitka Sound. All of them misspell his name. Keen died at Seattle in 1933.

The narrative is continued by P. Meigs in his diary:

"Jan. 13, Wed. We got under way this morning at 11:45 in spite of the rain, and started for Koutsnow. We have a large scow towing astern, filled with Indians, klootchmen, etc. It is wonderful how the miserable wretches stand the weather. Dropped anchor at Souley [Subia] Bay at 5:30 P.M."

"Jan. 14, Thurs. I was turned out of my hammock about one o'clock last night by hearing a horrible rumbling, like thunder, and seeing Dick hurrying on his pants, I jumped up and got on deck in short notice and just in time to hear the quartermaster give the sounding over the stern of 'one fathom', and as the ship draws about nine feet, there was but one conjecture left open to me as to the cause of the excitement, and that was that the ship was aground. Fortunately she slid right off, as soon as the engines were rung ahead; if she had not, we would have been in a tight place for the tide was falling rapidly. The wind had changed and caused her to swing inshore, and very much nearer than we thought she could. A kedge was gotten out astern and I turned in again with *much satisfaction*. Got underway again at 7:30 A.M. Anchored in Hood's Bay [Koteosok Anchorage], at 3 P.M.. About 1½ miles from Koutsnow.

"Jan. 15, Fri. Went with Mr. Pillsbury duck shooting but had no success. Dick went to Koutsnow and had a 'pow-wow' with the chiefs. Ducks two for 25 cts. [from the Indians?]"

The place names Kootznahoo, Koutsnow and Koteosok are used, with a variety of spellings, in the *Saginaw*'s deck log, in the Meigs diary and in the correspondence of both Commander Mitchell and Commander Meade. "Koutsnow," used above by Meigs, was the village later known as Kootznahoo and today as Angoon. It was, however, in some of the documents used as the name for the inlet today known as Kootznahoo. Koteosok Anchorage today is Killisnoo Harbor. Killisnoo, the name for both a small island that partly protects the harbor and for the village that stood on the island for many years, would seem to have been derived from "Koutswnow." A close relative, "Kenasnow" is preserved today as the name of a group of rocks near Killisnoo Island.

Meigs: "Jan. 16, Sat. An exploring party went up to the coal mine today, about 16 miles from here. They sounded and made a rough sketch of the channel which is filled with rocks and rapids, but Dick is going to try it in spite of all obstacles. They took only hard-tack with them and were consequently obliged to eat the smoked salmon of the Indians, which is not the cleanest stuff in the world. Tried the ducks again today with Mr. Little but shot none. We had the sun out nearly all day, making the air warm and everything look cheerful.

"Jan. 17, Sun. We dragged our anchor last night and had to let go another. Got under way at 8:30 A.M. with coal lighter in tow, and came to in Mitchell's Bay, Koutsnow Archipelago, at 12 noon. In coming here we had to pass two rapids, one quite near Koutsnow village, and the other several miles this way. Heavy squalls and rain all day.

"Jan. 18, Mon. Andre, a Koutsnow Indian and sort of pilot, came here with us from our last anchorage, and last night Dick gave him a dose of whiskey, setting him up *mightily*, and while he was feeling pretty happy he told us that his people did not feel friendly towards us when we first came, but that they are getting over it now. The coal mine is about a mile from here, but the channel to it is quite narrow, and if we were anchored there we would not be able to work the ship to any advantage if the 'painted devils' attempted to board us. The lighter was sent up to the mine to get the coal that was dug out by Mr. Ponte (about 25 tons). We had target practice today. Fired 30 lb. rifled guns and 24 lb. Howitzers, used Shrapnel and percussion shells. One shell burst just after leaving the gun; poor fuse, probably. After the firing, had all the guns loaded with canister (for the special benefit of the Indians). Snow and rain nearly all day."

The ship's log recorded: "Target practice with big guns. Miserable," according to Commander Meade, "except for the 30 pd. rifle in charge of Mids. Schroeder."

Meigs: "Jan. 19, Tues. I went with Mr. Pillsbury to the coal-mine this morning in the 3rd cutter, and met quite a nice little 'klootchman' there. She and I had quite a chat, considering the little knowledge I have of Chinook. I gave her tobacco, flattered her, etc., and when I left she waved her handkerchief and bowed as though she really wanted me to stay, but I said, 'Not for Joseph,' and I expect she said in return, 'Wake kumtux', ('I don't understand.') Very embarrassing position for a *bashful youth* like myself, to be placed in! There were five 'klootchmen' sitting around the fire, all seemingly pleased with my Chinook attempts, and the *pretty* one, before mentioned, making sheeps-eyes at me, but in spite of *all* obstacles, having warmed my feet and given away all my tobacco, I returned to the boat with my heart as well as ever. Two more nice little 'klootchmen' came alongside in the afternoon and I pleased them so well that they wanted mightily to come aboard and take a nearer look at me; but I told them the 'Tyee' (chief) said 'wake', (no). I gave a red blanket for a mountain sheep robe; value of the blanket $2.50. We had to duck the 'klootchmen' with buckets of water, tonight, to keep them away from the ship; there were about twelve canoes full of them, and they soon put for their camp-fires, probably insulted, disgusted and mad. Two of our men were just caught in a canoe under the bow; they had got ashore somehow and had come off again to smuggle some of the rest ashore, for a spree. The Capt. has just given orders to fire on any man attempting to leave the ship, so I imagine that will put an end to their larks. Pleasant all day!!!

"Jan. 20, Wed. *Rain. Rain! Rain!! All day!* We have about one pleasant day in ten. The men who tried to get ashore last night were put in double irons for five days and during that time they are allowed three biscuits and one pot of water per day. The Indians got all the coal on board yesterday, about 30 tons, and the wood, today, about 25 or 30 cords. A 'klootchman' brought a papoose alongside yesterday and when I asked her how much she would take for it, said, 'Quinam sitkum donner,' ('five half dollars'). Pretty cheap young one! Three 'klootchmen' came off in a canoe this morning. One of them was the best looking one I have seen yet. She had two or three silver bracelets on each arm, besides strings of beads, several silver rings on her fingers, and long strings of beads around her neck. I gave her tobacco and talked with her for a couple of hours. She was *really jolly*! She wanted me to go ashore but I said 'Wake', and then, supposing I could not go until a boat went, watched alongside until the 1st.

cutter went ashore for water, and when she saw them preparing to shove off, she called to me quite excitedly, and told me to go in the boat, but still I said 'Wake.' Then she tried her best to get me to go with her in the canoe but I 'couldn't see it.' At last she said she would go ashore and fix herself up fine and come on board the ship, but I told her the 'Tyhee' wouldn't let her. She seemed sorry, but not offended and when she went away, I kissed my hand to her, which pleased her mightily. If a poor chap was run after by the young ladies at home in this way, I don't know what would become of him.

"Jan 21, Thur. We paid the 'Siwashes' for the coal and wood today and the operation was quite interesting. Those who brought the coal were paid in coin at the rate of 11 4/10 cents per day, which was plenty. There were 32 or 33 in all and they only brought 30 tons of coal, and some of them swore they had worked 30 odd days, some 20, etc., they could not have worked very hard. Capt. Mitchell had left no written agreement as to how much they were to be paid, so we had considerable trouble. When we first came here Dick told them he would pay $2 per ton for all the coal there was out, but they thought he meant $2 per ton *for each man*, thus making the 30 tons cost over $1,800, and we had considerable difficulty to make the affair pass off quietly.

"We intended giving them axes, calicoes, etc., instead of coin but they said they would rather have the latter and then buy whatever they wanted. So the $60.-- was divided among them according to the number of days they had worked. As soon as they got the money they were quarrelsome, but we gave them good measure for their money in trade and they all seemed to be pretty well satisfied. All of the $60.-- and more came back to us in trade. The men got paid for the wood, 1 axe for 1½ cords or six yards of calico per cord. Also some tobacco for bringing it off. I jumped into a canoe this afternoon with a Siwash and Tenas Klootchman, paddled ashore and stayed in the various camps until after dark, talking to the dusky beauties. As night comes on they gather their families around their fires, and they seemed quite glad to have me take a seat in the ring. Dick thinks I am losing my heart, but I carry too powerful a guard in my mind and in my breast pocket.

"Jan. 22, Fri. We got underway at 1:45 P.M. and ran both rapids in safety, but it fairly made my hair stand on end. The tide was with us and we had to go at full speed to keep steerage way. In one place the water rushed over a little fall about 2 feet high, close alongside of us. Hell Gate, New York, is *nothing at all* compared to this. Andre brought the rest of the mining tools on board at Koutsnow. Dick has hired him with three other Indians and their canoe, to paddle back and forth from the Chilcat village, and is going to try to settle some difficulties between the Whites, the Koutsnows and the Chilcats. Left Koutsnow at 3:30 P.M. and dropped anchor in Fresh Water Bay at 8:10 P.M. The rush of a waterfall can be heard quite distinctly."

The *Saginaw* under Commander Mitchell had anchored here on July 31, 1868, and the name Freshwater Bay was entered in the ship's log. This indicates that Commander Mitchell probably named it, but the *Dictionary of Alaska Place Names* gives the credit for the naming to Commander Meade. The *Dictionary* says that Meade "gave the name only to Pavlof Harbor," a name that had been bestowed by the Russians some years earlier. Pavlof Harbor is apparently where the *Saginaw* anchored on both occasions.

Meigs: "Jan. 23, Sat. I went ashore in the cutter and gathered some leaves, moss, etc., and saw the fall. It is about 100 feet wide falls about 12 or 15 feet. The pilot says that in the summer the salmon jump up and down it in perfect swarms. The Indians have traps here to catch them in. Once, he says, he came here in a boat to get water, but they got so excited with the salmon that they filled their boat with them instead. They stood in the water about up to their knees and scooped the fish out with their hands. There are none here in the winter. I came near fainting today, I don't know why.

"Jan. 24, Sun. Got underway at 6:45 A.M. Ran all day before a howling south-easter and quite a heavy sea.

Passed a large glacier. Anchored in a lovely little bay with water-falls all around us, at 4:05 P.M. It is called William Henry Bay. The charts of these waters are very imperfect and incorrect. Had a little sunshine today. Thick and snowing now (5 P.M.)."

The *Dictionary of Alaska Place Names* says the name William Henry Bay was "obtained in 1869 by Comdr. Richard W. Meade, USN, from Hudson Bay traders." It is probable that he got it from the pilot, James W. Keen, but the origin of the name is unknown.

Meigs: "Jan. 25, Mon. Got underway at 7:23 A.M. and anchored at the mouth of Chilcat River at 1:20 P.M. We passed another glacier today; it was perfectly beautiful, (and cool). The land is much more rugged here near Chilcat and the mountains are covered with ice and snow right down to the water. A party went ashore this afternoon and saw the tracks of a bear. Blowing a gale from the N.W. all day, but the sun out and few clouds. (Cold!)

Commander Meade named the bay where they anchored Pyramid Island Harbor but this was later shortened to Pyramid Harbor, its present name. Pyramid Island is in the estuary off the mouth of the bay. Employees of the Hudson's Bay Company had called it Labouchere Bay for the company ship of that name. It was the *Labouchere* on which the pilot, James W. Keen, had served his apprenticeship and in which he had come to the Pacific Coast.

Meigs: "Jan. 26, Tues. I went ashore today and looked for the bear; got disgusted and attempted to climb the mountain. After a lot of hard work and several backslidings, risking my precious neck, I got within a few hundred yards of the top and getting a little scared, I started once more for the level ground, where I arrived in an amazingly short space of time, minus the seat of my pants! I sat down on a log to rest and to watch the squirrels, when I heard chopping, experienced a 'raising of the har' sensation and decamped in haste. Got some moss, etc. Pleasant all day but no sun.

"Jan. 27, Wed. Andre and his three Indians started for Chilkat, yesterday. The first village is six miles from here and the principal one about 25 miles. They are both on the Chilkat River which is very shoal and partly frozen over. Andre is to tell them that the row at Sitka originated through a mistake, and that we are friendly disposed. The Chilkats have more furs than any other tribe in these parts and we are anxious for them to come down and trade with us.

"Jan. 28, Thurs. Quite a party of us went ashore yesterday afternoon, and I had a search for my friends the squirrels, but could not find them. When I started for the ship again I set fire to an immense hollow tree, and it burned until midnight, making a beautiful fire. The flame rushed in a column from the top of it, about 70 feet from the ground, and the pitch trickled down its sides in sheets of flame. No sign of the Indians yet. Yesterday was the finest day we have had for months. Sunshine all day and a sunset as beautiful as anything I ever saw. The tops of the mountains looked like gold. Blowing hard today from the N.W. and quite cold. No sunshine!

"Jan. 29, Fri. Some of the Chilcats came down today, and I bought a black bear skin from one of them for a red blanket. Perry had a hunt yesterday but no luck. Saw plenty of mountain sheep tracks.

"Jan. 30, Sat. Got underway at 1:25 P.M. and left the Indians at Koutsnow at four o'clock of the morning of the 31st.

"Jan. 31, Sun. We had the most exciting time today that I have seen since I have been on the ship. It was while running through Peril Strait. We got through the first rapid successfully, but on reaching the second, we found the tide running against us so strong that we could not get ahead.

(Sketch.)

"When we got to the place marked 'A', we were struck by the tide on our port bow, which drove us in for the shore 'B' at a fearful rate. The helm was put hard a starboard but it had no effect whatever until we got so close I expected to hear her strike. We were making 23 revolutions and going like a streak. I could have snapped a bean ashore with ease. We all held our breaths for an instant, but sheered off. The tide was about ½ flood and ran about 11 knots an hour, (10 A.M.) We came to a standstill and hung there for 20 minutes, paddling as hard as we could and with all the steam the engines dared to have. Then she got a sheer to port and ran off in that direction and ran over to 'C', at the same time going astern. The helm was hard a port but she kept paying off more and more in spite of it. It was a frightful situation. The tide was rushing furiously over the rocks astern of us, making the water one mass of foam, and we were drawing nearer and nearer to it every moment. We had the foresail and foretopsail on her, the wind being astern, but nothing seemed to help us. All the officers were on deck and all said she was lost and expected every minute to see her go furiously into the breakers. Dick asked the engineer if he had all the steam he could carry and he said 'Yes.' 'Well,' said Dick, 'We must get out of here!' [Engineer] Fisher knew what he meant and had some Koutsnow coal thrown in; it is very inflammable and the steam rose at once. Our starboard boiler is weak and Fisher said things looked pretty 'scaly' down there when it got up to 23 pounds, (we have been running with never more than 15 or 16). At last Dick himself gave up and gave the order to furl the foresail, intending to turn suddenly and try to run her through. The Lord only knows what would have become of us if he had tried it. Fortunately at that moment a strong puff of wind came which, combined with the increased steam, helped us through and once more we breathed freely. I don't think I ever felt so thankful before in my life as when I saw her beginning to creep by the land and away from that beastly reef."

The above is a confusing account of the adventure. It must have happened in Sergius Narrows, but Meigs called it "the second rapids" which, traveling from the east, would have been Kakul Narrows. But the current is not nearly as strong in Kakul Narrows as in Sergius Narrows, so that any vessel able to buck through the latter would have no difficulty in Kakul Narrows.

Midshipman Seaton Schroeder, writing of the incident many years later, blamed the pilot for getting them into the difficulty.[1] Commander Meade, however, had been through Sergius Narrows twice previously and should have had some understanding of the current's velocity. Had the ship gone on the rocks he might well have been charged with unskillfulness. A prudent skipper, finding the current in the narrows that strong, would have eased off and drifted back to find an anchorage until slack water.

Meigs, continued: "We arrived at Sitka at 2:15 P.M. and found there had been a tremendous gale there. The Revenue Cutter 'Wayanda' had her bulwarks stove in and had to go to Victoria, so we missed that opportunity of sending letters.

"I did something very important yesterday, which I forgot to mention, viz., shave off my mustache. They made lots of fun of me saying I looked much older. We heard today of the murder of two traders by the Kake Indians."

The Meigs diary entry for February 2 will be found in Chapter 9.

"Feb. 3, Wed. I went ashore this morning to attend to some business, and then took a walk through the woods, on Gen. Davis' road, to Indian River, and gathered leaves, moss, etc. Everything was covered with snow, but the sun shone brightly *all day*, actually emitting warmth, melting the snow on the sunny side of the stumps and bringing to view the mosses, etc., beneath. It so invigorated me that I could fairly feel the blood coursing through my veins like a millrace. When I reached the River I found a tree fallen across it, upon which I stood for a long time, thinking of many of my dear friends and of the beauties of nature, the brook babbling beneath me like some laughing child. The Str. 'Otter' arrived in the evening from Victoria and to my almost uncontrollable joy brought us a large mail. I got 13 letters and two papers, the only letters I have received since I left Frisco. Full particulars of Uncle Richard's release, etc. It took me all evening to read my letters and I can safely say it was the pleasantest evening I have had on the 'Saginaw'.

"Feb. 4, Thurs. Busy all the morning copying official letters. Heavy snow and rain squalls in the afternoon.

"Feb. 5, Fri. Spent nearly all day writing. Nothing of interest took place.

"Feb. 6, Sat. Dick and I were invited to dine in the ward-room. Got the blues today, awfully, and headache. Had a jolly dinner in the ward-room; met Maj. and Mrs. [James O.] Woods, Lt. Eagen and his wife and Mrs. Kinkead.

"Feb. 7, Sun. Had muster and general order read on board in the morning, preventing me from going to church as I had intended."

According to the ship's log, the crew was mustered and the Articles of War were read. Was this part of the preparation for the foray against the Kake Indians, reported in the next chapter? Following that ceremony, a liberty party was allowed ashore.

Meigs: "Feb. 8, Mon. Sent letters on board the 'Otter'. To Mother, 1; Ed. Pratt, 1; Dallas Pratt, 1; Kittie Delafield, 1; Georgie Miller 1. Had a fancy dress ball on shore in the evening. Dick went but I didn't.

"Feb. 9, Tues. 'Otter' sailed for Victoria at 6 A.M. today. Sunday, Monday and today have *actually* been *cloudless* days and the jolly sunshine makes me long to be home. Perhaps I would be feeding the little snow-birds on the library plaza, where it shines so brightly."

NOTE

1. Seaton Schroeder, *A Half Century of Naval Service* (New York and London: D. Appleton, 1922), pp. 20-21.

IX

THE KAKE WAR

That is what some of the newspapers called it in the states and territories. There was no newspaper in Alaska at the time. It was a period when a main occupation of the U.S. Army was fighting Indians and any confrontation between whites and Indians in which more than two shots were fired was apt to be described in the papers as a war. What the Kake War amounted to was the death of two innocent white men, the death of one and perhaps two Kake Indians who probably were innocent, and the destruction of a lot of Indian property at the Kake villages.

The two unlucky white men were Ludwig Maager and William Walker. Maager had been a resident of Sitka since the fall of 1867 and owned some property in the town. Nothing is known of Walker except that in December 1868 he and Maager left Sitka in a large open boat to buy furs at some of the Indian villages. They were accompanied by Peter Peterhoff and Andre Andronska, both of mixed Russian-Tlingit blood. On the evening of January 13, 1869, the four men camped in a small cove, later named Murder Cove, near the southwest tip of Admiralty Island. It was the wrong place and the wrong time for their encampment.

In the meanwhile, about the end of the year 1868, a number of Southeast Alaska Tlingits had gathered at Sitka, perhaps for a potlatch. There were Chilkats and Kakes and perhaps others and, as related in Chapter 6, on New Year's night an altercation took place between some Chilkats and the Army sentinel or guard. The exact sequence of events after that is unclear. Commander Meade in his letter of

January 7, 1869, previously cited, said that a soldier and two Indians were dangerously wounded.[1]

The Indians were forbidden to leave and several canoes were fired on by a picket boat from the *Saginaw*. Frank K. Louthan, a Sitka merchant and trader, wrote that a Chilkat, a Kake and a Sitka Indian were killed. He added that both the Kakes and the Chilkats had applied to General Davis for compensation, in blankets, for the loss of their men but that it had been refused. He, Louthan, because he traded with the Chilkats and wanted to stay on good terms with them, satisfied their claim with 13 blankets.[2]

The Army version was given by Major General George H. Thomas, who visited Alaska in the summer of 1869: "In January last a party of Kake Indians attempted to leave Sitka in violation of orders; in resisting the attempt, one of the Indians was killed by a sentinel."[3]

Peveril Meigs, in his diary entry for January 5 (in Chapter 6) attributed the killing of one Indian, presumably a Kake Indian, to an Army foul-up. He wrote: "It seems that the officer of the guard, on shore, gave an order to the sentry on the wharf, not to allow any canoes to pass during the night. . . . This was to be in force during the night only, but the sentinel had no order to that effect, so he passed it to the relief, and in the morning a canoe with six or seven Indians attempted to pass, and when they only paddled faster when hailed by the sentinel, he fired into them four times, killing one and wounding one."

However it happened and whatever the reason, the Kakes left Sitka mad and determined to get revenge. They paddled through Peril Strait and down Chatham Strait and were starting to cross Frederick Sound toward their village or villages when they saw a campfire ashore on Admiralty Island. They investigated.

What happened next was reported by Commander Meade after he had talked with Peterhoff and Andronska, the two Russian-Indians:

> On the night of 13th Jan'y while encamped on shore in a small cove East of and near Point Gardner the traders were fired upon suddenly by a party of Kake Indians. Walker was instantly killed and Maager

> wounded. The latter fled to the brush but was pursued and dispatched with a knife. The Kakes having accomplished the deaths of two white men, left without molesting either Peterhoff or his comrade or the goods belonging to the white men, declaring that their object was revenge for a comrade killed at Sitka by a U.S. Soldier.
>
> The two Sitkas brought back all the property of the murdered men and I took them with me to identify the murderers in case I should be fortunate enough to catch them.[4]

P. Meigs also got a version of the murder, recorded in his diary on Tuesday, February 2: "Got the particulars of the murder today from Capt. Dempfel [Dimpfel], while I was on shore getting stores. It seems these two traders had two Sitkas with them and had camped for the night somewhere in Peril Straits. Their boat was drawn up and they were all asleep around their fire when suddenly a volley was fired right into them, and a party of Kakes rushed upon them and murdered the two whites, the two Sitkas escaping into the woods. The boat was capsized over the bodies and nothing was stolen, showing that it was done for revenge alone. Everyone expected that two whites would be killed to square for the two Siwashes we killed a short time ago. It seems very strange to me how the two Sitkas managed to escape so easily, and, although they brought the first news, I am almost inclined to think they are the murderers. They are a treacherous set of fiends. Of course the 'Saginaw' has got to go to Kake and try to find the guilty ones and hang them. We intend taking the two Sitkas with us to identify them. I expect that it will end in a fight and that we will knock their town down. I hope so!"

A third version of the events near Point Gardner on January 13, 1869, was reported by Capt. Thomas Gray, in command of Fort Wrangell, who got his information from a chief of the Stikine Indians:

> I have the honor to submit for the information of the Maj. General commanding the Dept. the following report of a sub chief of the Stikeen tribe, "Torryat," in reference to the murder of two white men and a Chinaman, said to have been committed by a Kake Indian,

"Coodick", about the 12th of Jan'y 1869, on Tootsmorth Island (Admiralty I'd.)

It appears from Torryat's statement that the brother of Coodick, a sub chief of the Kake tribe, was killed at Sitka about the 7th of Jan'y 1869, by the fire of one of the gunboats, while attempting to leave the harbor in a canoe during the evening or night: that Coodick applied to the Gen'l for presents or pay for his brother's death, which was refused him, and the Indian left vowing to "get even" on the first opportunity. He left Sitka with the body of his brother, accompanied by five canoes of Sitka Indians. When they reached Tootsmorth Island, distant about 18 miles from Kake, they saw a fire and a tent on the shore: the canoe containing the Kake Indians immediately paddled for the shore and on arriving there, Coodick, seeing a white man standing near the camp-fire, immediately drew his pistol to shoot him, the pistol missing fire, he rushed on him with his war knife and stabbed him in the left breast; the white man making an effort, got away, when Coodick, seeing an old man sitting in the tent, sprang upon him and stabbed him, repeating the blows until he was quite dead. The younger man who had been first attacked, ran a short distance on the beach and fell, when the Sitka Indians, who had landed by this time, came up to him and finished the work so well commenced. Torryat says that the Kake Indians would take no part of the plunder found in the tent of the murdered men and that the Sitkas took it all -- giving 1/3 part of the goods, etc. to the guide of the white party, a Sitka Indian, who was rather a young man, speaking a little Chinook. The Chinaman ran away as soon as the attack was made, and, though nothing positive was known about him, yet the inference is that he also was murdered. After the Indians had completed their work, they wrapped the bodies up in their blankets, and hauling the boat up on the beach, above high-water mark, they made it fast, placing the bodies alongside of it. The murdered men were doubtless on a trading expedition, as they had a general assortment of goods with them. When Torryat saw the Sitka Indians they had some forty gallons of whiskey with them but he did not learn where the liquor came from. They had also in their possession a Henry Rifle and a revolver, belonging to the murdered white men. The older man they described as being about forty years of age, five feet 10 inches in height, with a gray beard; the other man was younger,

> of medium size, quite good looking, and wore a sort of uniform with shoulder straps on his coat. From the description given of the men and the goods, it is supposed that they are the men who purchased a boat from the "Otter" when last at Sitka, the one picked up from the wreck of the schooner, and that the goods belonged to Mes's Schirpser & Co. of Sitka. The name of the older man is supposed to be "Toby." The name of the Sitka guide could not be ascertained. I would add that Torryat said that propositions had been made to him by the Kakes in presence of the Sitka Indians, to form a league for the purpose of destroying all the military posts within this Dept., which overtures were rejected by Torryat on behalf of the Stikeen Tribe.[5]

Meigs, in including the letter in his diary, said: "I here give a copy of a letter to Gen. Davis, some of the particulars of which are incorrect, but it will give some idea of the manner in which Walker and Maager were murdered. We have no idea that the Sitkas had any hand in it whatever!

"The 'Chinaman' referred to in this letter, instead of having been murdered, is now working with the 'Sitka guide' on board of this vessel, having both shipped as Landsmen. The supposed 'Chinaman' is a Sitka Siwash. It is all a mistake about the goods having been divided, for the two Sitkas brought them *all* back to Mess. Schirpser & Co., the 'Henry rifle' included."

It may be worth noting that the Stikine and Sitka tribes of the Tlingits had been at war for many years. "Torryat" may have embellished the account he gave Captain Gray in a way to defame the rival tribe.

The decision of Commander Meade to go after the Kake murderers was probably not a difficult one. Anthropologists distinguish between two groups of Natives living on the south side of Frederick Sound as Kakes and Kuyu but in the popular mind they were all Kakes and the Kakes had acquired a reputation as marauders and terrorists. The reputation extended clear to Puget Sound. For years, perhaps for generations, groups of Indians from Southeastern Alaska and British Columbia had traveled to Puget Sound to trade, plunder, acquire slaves, or perhaps just to see the country. After settlement of the Puget Sound area by whites, the Indians also hired out to pick hops.

The coming of the whites brought not only some jobs for Indians but conflict between whites and Indians, both resident and visiting. U.S. warships came to the Sound to try to keep peace. In 1856 a large number of Indians, including some Kakes, camped on the outskirts of the settlement of Port Gamble. When they became disorderly the settlers appealed to the captain of the USS *Massachusetts*. In the encounter that followed a Kake chief was killed. The rest of the Kakes returned home, but they did not stay there.

On the night of August 11, 1857, a war party of Kakes landed at the farm of Isaac N. Ebey on Whidbey Island. He had served as Collector of Customs for the district and the Indians considered him equal in rank to the dead chief. They killed Ebey and cut off his head and took it home with them. That branded the Kakes as villains incarnate, and the fact that Ebey's head, or perhaps only the scalp, was retrieved by a Hudson's Bay Company trader some time later and returned to the Ebey family did not erase that image.[6]

The next black mark against the Kakes in general came in 1865 when the British trading schooner *Royal Charley*, out of Victoria, was attacked in Alaska waters. The four white men on board were killed and p1827Xhel was plundered and destroyed.[7]

In the light of those past events, Commander Meade undoubtedly had no compunctions about preparing for a full scale operation against the Kake villages.

On Wednesday, February 10, the *Saginaw*'s log reported that between 4 and 6 P.M. 15 privates and two non-commissioned officers from the garrison on shore came aboard with arms, ammunition and rations for seven days. At 8 P.M. General J. C. Davis, his aide-de-camp Captain Samuel B,. Mclntire, Captain John Henriques of the U.S. Revenue Marine Service, and Captain Charles Bryant, a special agent of the Treasury Department, also came on board.

Meigs, in his diary entry for February 10, added: "We have on board the two Indians that were with the traders when they were murdered, and two Sitkas who heard the Kakes swear that they would kill the whites if they got a chance."

The *Saginaw* left Sitka at 7:05 A.M. on February 11 and at 9 went aground on gravelly bottom in Whitestone

Narrows. A kedge anchor was used to get her off and she proceeded into Peril Strait and "after passing 2nd rapids, at 12 m. stopped to speak a canoe. Took on board the bodies of Ludwig Maager and Wm. Walker, killed by a party of Indians. At 1 P.M. sent bodies to Sitka."

In his letter of February 24 to Admiral Craven, Commander Meade wrote:

> On the 11th while passing through Peril Strait I met the canoe which had been sent to Pt. Gardner to bring in the bodies of the unfortunate men.
>
> I caused an inspection to be made of the remains which were in a shocking condition. Though they had been interred by the Sitkas, the wolves and crows had eaten the flesh from the bones, leaving but a foot and a leg and some shreds of clothing. The leg was identified as Maager's and the terrible gash in the calf sufficiently verified the truth of the report as to the manner in which they had been "finished".[8]

Meigs: "Feb. 11, Thur. Got underway at 7 A.M. Took ground twice and met, in Peril St's, the party of Indians with the bodies. There was very little left of them but bones; their feet were perfect and one of them had the calf of the left leg with an immense gash, made by a large knife, in it and extending clear through. The bones were so gnawed by wolves, etc. that it was impossible to find any other marks of violence. The mens names were Ludwig Maager and Wm. Walker. Came to anchor at 1:15 P.M. I forget to say that the knife wound had been bound up, tending to prove what the Indians told us, that he lived for a day after being wounded. After an examination, we sent the bodies on to Sitka.

"Feb. 12, Fri. Got underway at 7 A.M. and let go anchor Koteosok Harbor, inside of Kenasnow I'd at 1:05 P.M. Indians from Koutsnow came around us at once. Had quite a serenade from a party of klootchmen on shore, about nine or ten o'clock in the evening.

"Feb. 13, Sat. Got underway at 5:35 A.M. and after a short delay at Koutsnow, on account of the tide, passed through the first rapids without accident and anchored just above and took on board a deck-load of wood which the Siwashes had already cut, by Dick's order. I went in the dingy with Gen'l Davis, Capt. Bryant, Capt. Henriques and several others to Koutsnow Village. We visited most of the chief huts and were well received. I recognized some of my old 'tillicums' ('friends') among the klootchmen and bought three small boxes from them for 75 cts. The huts are generally built square, roofed over except in the centre, where there is an opening of about 6 feet square for the smoke to get out. They have the fire on the ground, directly under this opening. The bunks are built all around the sides of the building and are generally well supplied with skins, blankets, Vermin, etc. In one of the houses a klootchman was blacking her face and kindly offered to perform the same operation on mine. I took off my hat and bent down as though I was going to have it done and she laughed like fun, but I backed out, much to her disappointment. When we were returning we found a party assembled around a large fire in which they were burning a body; they made the most doleful noises but nary a tear was shed that I could see.

"Feb. 14, Sun. Got up this morning with a dull, aching pain in my knee, which brought back all my melancholy thoughts on that subject. O God! How it draws down all my hopes. Very rainy all day. Got underway at 8:35 A.M.; got through the rapids in safety and shaped our course for Kake, Saginaw Bay, where we arrived at 6:45 P.M. and found that all but one of the houses, in the small village, to which we were opposite, were deserted by the Indians and left with the doors locked. Pilot Keene went ashore and had a pow-wow with the Indian that remained and found that *one* of the murderers had gone towards Victoria and the other was probably somewhere near the principal Kake village, not far from here. A confab was held in the cabin and it was determined to send a party on shore and destroy all the houses that were deserted, leaving the one that was occupied, giving them to understand that the same thing will be done again if they allow any murderers to escape hereafter. I have got permission to go with the party.

"Feb. 15, Mon. 10 A.M. I have just returned on board. At 8 o'clock the 1st cutter was called away, taking besides its crew, six of Gen'l Davis' men, the pilot, and your humble serv't, all under the command of Mr. Pillsbury. We landed just to the right of the village, picketed the soldiers between the houses and the woods and then set to work with coal and alcohol and '*von leetle* match' and soon had one of the shanties in flames. Shickshaney, a Tyhee's daughter, was allowed to retain her house, two canoes and some articles that belonged to her, but all the rest, (5 houses and 6 canoes) were entirely destroyed. These houses are about 30 feet square and built of planks about 3 inches thick, hewn out of logs, so when we had them all lit it made quite a fine bonfire. We heard the Indians in the woods yell several times, and their dogs would bark every now and then, but they were afraid to molest us. I felt sorry for Shickshaney. She is quite a pretty klootchman and I believe has been the mistress of nearly every officer that has visited here. Capt. _____ [Mitchell?] carried her around in the 'Saginaw' for a long time. When she saw the buildings all in flames, she cried like fun. Dick, on the ship, heard the Indians yell and immediately had the guns trained on the place where he expected to see them make their appearance. I had a carbine, a cutlass and my revolver and was quite ready for a fight. Got underway again at 9:45 A.M. leaving the houses in full blast and the bunch of natives, consisting of about 8 women, 2 men and 3 or 4 children, looking on the mass of desolation in a decidedly forlorn manner. Shickshaney stood with her handkerchief, (*a clean one*) to her eyes, but, I have no doubt vowing vengeance in her heart."

Despite the misgivings Meigs felt about Shickshaney, a year later she reciprocated for the consideration shown her by the *Saginaw* crew. On a trip from Kake to Sitka she stopped at the village of Neltushkin where she learned that a white man, Frank Mahoney, was being held prisoner. He was from the trading schooner *Langley*, wrecked near Neltushkin, and the vessel's skipper, Michael Sullivan, was being held at Kootznahoo Village. When Shickshaney got to Sitka she informed Collector of Customs William Kapus of the circumstances. A joint Army-Navy operation used a steam launch from the USS *Cyane* to rescue the two men. Sullivan, incidentally, was the same man who had been rescued by the *Saginaw* in 1868 from the wrecked *Louisa Downs*.[9]

Commander Meade wrote on February 24:

> On the 15th proceeded to Kupreanoff I. and utterly destroyed the largest Kekon village. This place (Lat. 56°56′30″ N. and Long. 133°49′ W.) was also found to be deserted by every living soul.[10]

If Commander Meade's coordinates are correct, the destroyed village was somewhat south of the present village of Kake, perhaps at the entrance to Hamilton Bay where Meigs put it.

Meigs, February 15, continued: "Let go anchor in front of Kake, Hamilton Bay, at about noon; found the place *entirely* deserted; the houses locked and not a living thing to be seen, save a dog. There were 13 houses here, averaging 40 feet square, and built much better than those just destroyed. We fired five shells from the 30 lb. Parrots and then sent the 1st cutter on shore with the soldiers. Much to my disgust, Dick wouldn't let me go! Flames issued from the first house at 1:05 and about 2 minutes later 2 more on fire. At 2 o'clock the whole village was wrapped in flames. The cutter returned at 2:10. Got underway at 2:35 P.M. after firing two more shells, and shaped our course for the village we burned this morning, where we arrived at 5:10 P.M. Shickshaney was brought on board and a long consultation took place in the cabin, and as I was on deck I do not know *all* that transpired, but she said that one of the murderers was in another of the Kake villages not far from here and that vengeance was vowed against any boat that attempted to land there, but I guess we will see about that tomorrow! I rather think _____ [Meade?] took a fancy to the Tyhee's daughter. It takes the Siwashes two or three months to build a house, and they cost 200 to 300 blankets apiece. We burned today 18 houses and destroyed 7 canoes; also 'hiu salmon' (dried). The Hyda chief we have on board was delighted with the havoc and said, 'Kake Siwash wake kiosh! Hyas clahowya *alta*!' ('Kake Indians are no good! They are very poor now!') The men are very much disgusted because the Indians would not fight, but I hope we will have a brush with them tomorrow.

"Got underway at 8:40 A.M. and arrived at another small village of 8 or 10 houses at about 10:15 A.M. [This was in Snug Harbor, according to the ship's log; in Security Bay according to Meade.] The place was deserted and the same old tune was played again. After spreading the splinters in every direction by the aid of a few shells, we set fire to the place at 11:15 and at 11:54 the cutter returned, leaving the entire village in flames. There is not a living thing to be seen. The Lord only knows where the Indians have all gone to. Two boats were off about ½ the day, cutting around in the various inlets in search of them; they found two old log forts, which they destroyed, but nary a Siwash to be seen anywhere."

Midshipman J. E. Pillsbury, in a report to Commander Meade, wrote:

> On the 16th at 11 A.M. I landed at Tom's ranche on Kou Id. with seven seamen and sixteen soldiers. I destroyed ten houses and one canoe and returned to the ship at 11:50 A.M.
>
> At Kekon [Kupreanof I.] and at Tom's ranche I found iron work and chains which evidently originally belonged to some vessel.[11]

Midshipman E. W. Bridge also made a written report to Commander Meade:

> In obedience to orders to proceed to the head of Security Bay and make search for and destroy, if possible, an Indian village said to be located there, I left the ship at 1:30 P.M. on the 16th with an armed force in two boats, consisting of 17 seamen and 15 soldiers. I found two stockaded forts and one fishing ranche at the head of the bay, a distance of about 5 miles from our anchorage. The forts were about 100 feet square, from 15 to 17 feet high and built of logs from 9 to 15 inches thick. These, with the ranche, I completely destroyed. They had apparently been deserted some time.
>
> I found a good channel to within a mile of the forts, the water from 4½ to 9 fathoms in depth. I returned to the ship at 4:30 P.M.[12]

Commander Meade included some Alaska geography in his letter of February 26 to Admiral Craven:

In our recent cruise to the Kake or Kekon country we entered a bay on the NW end of Kou Island which from its great advantages as a harbor I named Security Bay and the anchorage near Tom's ranche Snug Harbor. The bay is about 6½ miles in extent and has an average depth of water of 10 fathoms to the anchorage and from 9 to 3 fathoms everywhere else. The rise and fall of the tide is about 14 feet.

A number of fresh water streams empty into the bay and in season the salmon, cod and other fish are said to abound, while the growth of cedar, hemlock and pine timbers is inexhaustible.

Outside of Security Bay is a good roadstead with 10 to 12 fathoms, soft bottom, and perfectly sheltered from SE winds. Any sailing vessel may enter Snug Harbor and the bay will shelter a large number of vessels. Snug Harbor has a southern exposure, is tolerably well cleared and is one of the salmon fishing sites of the Kake Indians. It is perfectly land-locked.

The whales are said to resort to Chatham Strait in the calving season and, if so, Security Bay is the best rendezvous possible for a whaling fleet. As a harbor it is immensely superior to Sitka and is a better site for a military post than is Kootznahoo. A sailing vessel making Cape Ommaney with a S. Easterly wind can be at anchor in a few hours in the outer roads of Security Bay without requiring a pilot.

Security Bay is a few miles west of Saginaw Bay, named and examined by Commander Mitchell and selected by General Halleck as the site for a military post. Saginaw Bay has none of the advantages of Security Bay, being rather open and the anchorage ground fringed with rocks. As far as my knowledge extends, no vessel of war has ever before entered Security Bay though the Hudson Bay Co's. steamers have long resorted to it and are well aware of its advantages.

We have cruised a great deal in this part of Alaska and my experience convinces me that Security Bay is the best and most accessible harbor that the Koloshian Archipelago affords.[13]

In addition to naming Security Bay and Snug Harbor, Commander Meade named Retaliation Point, Flat Island, Cedar Island, Harbor Island, Cleft Island and Indian Rock, all of them in Security Bay. All of them are on the chart today, but Snug Harbor is not. There are four Snug Harbors in Alaska but none in Security Bay. It might be noted, too, that when Commander Meade named Security Bay the "best and most accessible" harbor in what was then known as the Koloshian (Indian) Archipelago, he had visited fewer than a dozen of the many harbors in what is now called the Alexander Archipelago.

NOTES

1. Meade Letterbook, pp 29-30.

2. "Report from F. K. Loutham on the Indian Tribes of Alaska (October 28, 1869)," Appendix E in *Letter of the Secretary of the Interior communicating in compliance so much of the report of Vincent Colyer, special Indian commissioner, as relates to the Indian village of Wrangel, Alaska, showing the condition of that village previous to its recent bombardment by United States troops*, Senate Ex. Doc. No. 68, 41st Congress, 2d Session, pp. 16-18.

3. Report dated September 27, 1869 in *Annual Report of the Secretary of War for 1869*, House Ex. Doc. 1, pt. 2, v. 2, 41st Congress, 2d Session.

4. Dated at Sitka, February 24, 1869. Meade Letter book, p. 4.

5. Dated at Fort Wrangel, February 3rd, 1869, and addressed to Capt. S. B. MacIntire, at Sitka. A copy is included in the Meigs diary with the March 15 entry.

6. Hubert Howe Bancroft, *History of Washington, Idaho and Montana.* Vol. 27 of *History of the Pacific States* (San Francisco: A. L. Bancroft, 1890), p. 137.

7. E. W. Wright, ed., *Lewis and Dryden's Marine History of the Pacific Northwest* (New York: Antiquarian Press, 1961), p. 144.

8. Meade Letterbook p. 50.

9. William Kapus, Collector of Customs, Sitka, to George S. Boutwell, Secretary of the Treasury, February 23, 1870, in U.S. Customs Service records, Alaska Historical Library, Juneau.

10. Meade Letterbook, p. 51.

11. Meade Letterbook, p. 55.

12. Meade Letterbook, pp. 55-56.

13. Meade Letterbook, pp. 56-59.

X

THE LAST WEEKS OF THE CRUISE

After the destruction of the Kake villages the *Saginaw*, with General Davis, Major McIntire, Captain Henriques and Captain Bryant still aboard, made a visit to the coal mine at Kootznahoo Inlet. While there Commander Meade honored the general by giving the name Davis Creek to the waterway connecting Mitchell Bay and Kanalku Bay. The ship dropped anchor at Sitka at 4 P.M. on February 23 after an absence of 12 days.

The ship's log on February 10 had recorded that 17 enlisted man had arrived aboard with rations for 7 days. Presumably they were fed from Navy stores on the other five days of the cruise.

Meigs: "Feb. 23. Arrived at Sitka at 4 P.M. *Oh what ecstasy*! Capt. Henriques of the U.S. Revenue Cutter 'Reliance' sent us a box of apples; they look like old times!

"Feb. 24, Wed. Rain! Rain! Rain! Spent the day in the cabin, writing letters.

"Feb. 25, Thur. Sent a letter to Charlie; also one to Ed. Bodine. Rain! Rain! Rain! *Rain*! Capt. Henriques sent us a keg of beer. Mrs. Kinkead sent Dick and me each a little moss cross.

"Feb. 26, Fri. Nothing of importance.

"Feb. 27, Sat. My 22nd birthday! Rained like fury all day. Went ashore with Bridge and had a little billiards -- then spent the evening with Mr. Little at Mrs. Kinkead's. Had a jolly time! Met at Mrs. K's the unmarried American lady of Sitka -- Miss. Messer. She is very pleasant! [Mr. Little was a Midshipman in the *Saginaw*.

Miss Addie Messer was the first teacher in the public school established by the City of Sitka.]

"Feb. 28, Sun. Cleared off at last.

"Mar. 1, Mon. Went ashore with Bridge to take observations, but the sun shut himself in as usual.

"Mar. 2, Tues. Went on the Gov't I'd [Japonski] and had a little walk. Got a horn to make a powder horn of. This has been, without exception, the pleasantest day we have had since we have been here. Dick and I took a walk with Gen. Davis, to Indian River. It is a very romantic place and, in season, is full of salmon and trout. Capt. Dempfel [Dimpfel] and Mr. Louthen [Louthan] had a knock-down fight last night. Dempfel got the worse of it! [Dimpfel was in charge of the Quartermaster Department at Sitka; Frank Louthan was a merchant, a partner of John Kinkead].

"The Army officers here are in a perfect mess; they have all reported each other for various things, and there is going to be a court-martial soon to investigate matters. They are about as drunken a set as I ever saw. [Meigs' opinion of the Army at Sitka was shared by many others who have written about it.]

"Mar. 3, Wed. The Str. 'John L. Stephens' came in this A.M. with stores for the Army, and I accompanied Mid'm Schroeder, in the 3rd cutter, when he went for our mail. We had great difficulty in getting to her, owing to the wind. We all got drenched, and when we at last got alongside, they told us our mail had gone to the Revenue Cutter 'Reliance' so we turned back half in disgust and half in joy at our luck. When I got on board I found thirteen letters awaiting their happy owner. Ma's Christmas box has come at last and I am delighted with it. It contained a lovely little hand-glass, a napkin ring and a pincushion from Ma.; a little tablet from Julia and a case of writing materials from Kittie Delafield. I got one letter from Jim Truslow; from Dick Delafield, 1; J. B. Pratt, 1; Hal. Meigs, 1; Carrie Cook, 1; Kittie Delafield, 1; Louise, 1; Katie, 1; Julia, 1; Father, 1; *Mother, 3.* It came on to blow last night, a perfect gale from N.E. and still continues. It is perfectly awful. The gusts seem to come down the sides of the mountains *like lead* and I believe I have had several teeth blown down my throat. We are riding at two hawsers and two anchors, and have steam up. We had to change our berth this afternoon. The Str. 'George S. Wright' came in today with the members of the court-martial that is to be held here.

"Mar. 4, Thur. Inauguration Day. Hurrah for Grant!!! Staid on board all day. Still blowing hard!

"Mar. 5, Fri. In the afternoon we hauled alongside the 'Wright' and commenced coaling. Capt. Henriques spent the evening with us.

"Mar. 6, Sat. The 'Stephens' has been seized for violating the Revenue laws by landing goods at Tongass and Wrangel."

The *John L. Stephens* was seized at Sitka on March 4, 1869, by Collector of Customs Hiram Ketchum. She had sailed from San Francisco with cargo for Tongass, Wrangell and Sitka and on the way up had stopped at Victoria where she loaded a quantity of flour. Some of the flour was sold at each Tongass and Wrangell but was unloaded there without permits from the Customs officers stationed at those ports. Liquor was also unloaded at both ports in violation of the Revenue Laws. The *Stephens* was sent to San Francisco in charge of a prize crew consisting of Lieut. M. A. Healy, Quartermaster Joseph Crawford and Seaman Daniel Green, all of the Revenue Marine Service. Lieut. Healy was to have a long career in Alaska waters in command of the Revenue Cutter *Bear*, gaining the nickname "Hell Roaring Mike."

Meigs, continued: "I forgot to say that Shickshaney has been in Sitka for some time. She is afraid to live in Kake. She also said that the two Kake murderers came to her house soon after we burned the village. We finished coaling today. Took in about 66 tons.

"Mar. 7, Sun. Went on deck this morning and was quite surprised to find that it was *Sunday*. I believe I never did such a thing before, but the days are so much alike here that I am not much to blame. Had to go back to the cabin and put on my 'Sunday-go-to-meetings' for muster. Staid all day in the cabin writing letters.

"Mar. 8, Mon. I have been troubled for several days with rheumatism in my right shoulder. I expect to be an old man by the time I am thirty years of age!

"Mar. 9, Tues. A court-martial was held on board this morning for the trial of Geo. Prouten, Sailmaker's Mate, for insolence. I went ashore with Dick in the afternoon and beat him two games of billiards. Took a walk on the beach. I am sick of this beastly journal!!!!

"Mar. 10, Wed. We sent our letters on board the 'Stephens' today. I was very busy *all day* copying Dick's letters, Remark-book, etc. Rain all day.

"Mar. 11, Thur. The steamer 'Wright' left here this morning for Victoria via Fort Tongass. The 'Stephens' did not sail owing to the thickness of the weather.

"Mar. 12, Fri. Rain! Rain! Rain! Rain! Rain! Rain!!! 'Stephens' sailed today while I was at the Club House.

"Mar. 13, Sat. Went this morning with Dick to see the Greek service performed. There is much more mummery in it than in the Roman Catholic; nothing but chanting, kissing, burning of incense, etc., the congregation kissing the floor at intervals. Took a walk.

"Mar. 14, Sun. Went to hear Parson Raynor for the first time. Was not edified! Walked with Dick to Indian River. It being a *remarkably* fine day, we saw everybody out, and the liberty men were having a gay time with the klootchmen, dancing and all kinds of carrying on. Spent the afternoon at Maj. Wood's with Dick. Went ashore with Bridge in the evening and made several jolly calls.

"Mar. 15, Mon. Making preparations for leaving this *lovely* place. I went ashore to see about some small stores, etc., in the morning. In the afternoon the Hyda Tyhee came on board with his Klootchman and three Indians. [The ship's log reported that 6 Indians came aboard for passage to "Kazan."] Gen'l Davis sent 15 men on board in the evening.

"Mar. 16, Tues. Got underway at 6:03 A.M. and spent all the forenoon in stopping canoes that we met in Peril Sts. etc. Those Indian that were posted hoisted the white flag as soon as they saw us. We examined over a dozen canoe loads of inhumanity but found nary a Kake. We had to fire a shell ahead of four canoes to let them know that we wished to see them alongside. I need hardly say that it had the desired effect. We stopped for a few minutes at Kootznahoo to hear about the fight they had among themselves, (4:50 P.M.) and then proceeded right on up Chatham Sts."

At 4 A.M. on Wednesday, March 17, the *Saginaw* was rounding Point Retreat and heading down what they called Takou Strait. At 8 o'clock the ship was standing in toward Auk Village and at 8:10 it came to off the village of 14 houses. This was the Auk village in Admiralty Cove, Youngs Bay, long since abandoned. The ship anchored in Taku Harbor that night, then went on to the Indian village of Sumdum in Holkham Bay.

Meigs: "Mar. 17, Wed. Remained only a few minutes [at Auke] and went right on for Tako, where we arrived at 12:15 P.M. At the mouth of the Tako River, in Stevens' Channel, we saw quite a number of small icebergs. It blew very hard all last night, and we had quite a heavy sea. On arriving at Tako we found nary a Siwash, they having all gone hunting. Took a sail in the 3rd cutter.

"Mar. 18, Thur. Got underway at 8:47 A.M. and ran on through Stephen's Chl. to Tsumdan [Sumdum] where we arrived at 12:07 P.M. The Indians were afraid to come on board at first, but we gave them to understand that we were friendly, and quite a number of them came on board. They are, I believe, renegades from various tribes, principally of the Tarkoos. They are the finest looking savages I have seen yet; appear to be well off, and all dress remarkably well. They have much handsomer furs than any tribe we have visited, but they want a blanket for each Marten skin, which is too much. Their Hyas Tyhee was dressed in real Indian style; all his clothes were of skins, very handsomely decorated with beads. He had eyes *exactly* like Uncle Martin Schenck.

"We fired a percussion shell from one of our 30 lb rifles, which surprised them very much. They also admired my 7 shooter. One of them saw the end of a revolver in my pocket and said to me, 'Okoak wake klosh. Nika halo tenass musket!' which being interpreted is, 'That is not good. *I* have not got any pistol.' He then threw open his blanket for me to see, and right away asked for tobacco, which I gave him. Our Hydah Tyee was quite sick in the evening and night, and I gave him whiskey. He was in great pain with something like rheumatism and when his suffering was more than he could bear, he would throw his arms around his klootchman's neck, drag himself half out of bed and moan awfully. I felt ever so sorry for him as he is without exception the best Indian I have seen; he seems to like me, too.

"Mar. 19, Fri. Took the old Hydah some more whiskey & some cake, which pleased him. Got underway at 2:45 P.M. Everybody in a bad humor! Lots of icebergs floating around. Saw, indistinctly, a lunar rainbow. Saw it afterwards *very* distinctly.

"Mar. 20, Sat. We laid off Cape Fanshaw a part of last night but resumed our course at daylight. At 12:40 we ran aground in Wrangel Narrows; no damage done, (mud flat.) Had to come to at 3:40 P.M. & wait for next low water. It has been a lovely day and the moon is now shining brightly, reminding me of happy times long past. (We ran aground *twice* today.)

"Mar. 21, Sun. Got underway at 11:45 A.M. and let go anchor at Wrangel at 5 P.M. Hi-u Siwash! Hi-u klootchmen! Took a good row in the dingy. Beautiful day and lovely moonlight night.

"Mar. 22, Mon. Unpleasant all day. Didn't go ashore. Read over some old letters and was generally spooney."

On the 22nd the ship's log reported that 13 soldiers, a corporal and a sergeant had left the ship for the post ashore. The log had reported that this number of Army personnel came aboard at Sitka on March 15. But when the ship reached Fort Tongass on the 27th, "13 soldiers and 2 non-commissioned officers" also left the ship there although their boarding had not been reported.

Meigs: "Mar. 23, Tue. Got underway at 9 A.M., having on board Capt. [W.] Borrowe and his son. We went to find a passage through Souchoi Ch'l [Dry Strait] but were unsuccessful. Returned to Wrangel at 5:20 P.M. Raining all day.

"Mar. 24, Wed. Took on board our mail and left Wrangel at 1:15 P.M. We are now, (9 P.M.), running in Duke of Clarence Sts. Raining and blowing all day.

"Mar. 25, Thurs. Came to at the salmon fishery of Vincent Baranovitch, at Casan, at 4 A.M., blowing hard, raining and hailing. Spent about half the day ashore among the Indians. The salmon make their appearance in the middle of May, and do not disappear until September, and during the fishing season they are so numerous here that it is difficult to navigate the small streams in canoes, owning to the quantity of fish. They tell me that by putting a nail in the end of a small stick you can spear as many as you wish, in fact they say you can hardly thrust the stick into the water without striking a fish.

"Mar. 26, Fri. Went with Mr. Pillsbury and Mr. Little after ducks. Got only four. We saw great numbers of geese but we couldn't get at them. Our Hydah Tyee left here today.

"Mar. 27, Fri. Got underway at 4:25 A.M. having on board Offutt & '*his family*.'

"Will leave them at Tongas. Arrived at Tongas at 5:05 P.M. Disembarked the soldiers.

"Mar. 28, Sun. Left Tongas at 6 A.M. & arrived at Fort Simpson [a Hudson's Bay Company post] at 9:25 A.M. We are once more in British Territory. Liberty party went ashore. An Englishman here sent Dick a lot of Vulcan [Eulachon] or Candle-fish, so called because when dry, they will burn like a candle. This is the largest Indian settlement we have seen yet.

"Mar. 29, Mon. Left Fort Simpson at 4:25 A.M. *Beautiful day*.

"Mar. 30, Tues. We ran all night and got off our course twice. We got mixed up among some islands this morning and lost some time. Anchored at Bella Bella at 10:40 A.M. and being short of coal took on board about 15 cords of wood. Left Bella Bella at 1:23 P.M. I gave ½ dollar for an Indian paddle. For several days I have seen seals. Pleasant! Came in to Safety Cove (on the edge of Queen Charlotte Sd.) at 7 P.M.

"Mar. 31, Wed. Got underway at 4:30 A.M.; ran across Queen Charlotte Sd. in the teeth of a gale and came to at Ft. Rupert at 3:25 P.M.

"April 1, Thurs. Got underway at 5:25 A.M. and are now, (10 P.M.), running in Sts. of Georgia. Rain all day. Arrived at Nanaimo at 6 A.M. Took in 96 tons of coal.

"April 2, Fri. Rode on locomotive nearly all day. Eggs *3* bitts per doz!

"April 3, Sat. Left Nanaimo at 4:30 A.M. Met British gunboat 'Forward' at 1:35 P.M. At 12½ P.M. we were opposite San Juan Id. Arrived at Victoria at 2:35 P.M. Went ashore and weighed myself; weight 161½ lbs., gained 1½ lbs. since leaving Sitka. Spent evening ashore etc.

"April 4, Sun. Took Communion at English church; enjoyed the service *immensely*. Was with Dick. We took a long walk over Beacon Hill! Lots of flowers in bloom; ditto girls out walking. The humming of the bees is delicious. Snow peaks in distance! Nice and warm here; seems like Heaven!

"April 5, Mon. Went with Bridge, in the evening, to drive. Visited Esquimalt & Beacon Hill. Had pretty gay time. Got on board bet. 11 & 12 and turned in about 1.

"April 6, Tues. I forgot to say that Str. 'Active' brought news for us yesterday. It seems that a mail went up to Sitka on the 'Constantine' for us, an official letter, in which, ordered us to Frisco. There is a rumor that the 'Saginaw' is to be put out of commission and if so, Dick will probably be ordered home and I will have to go too. Don't like it! We rec'd a telegram yesterday ordering us to Frisco. Will probably leave here in a few days. I am sick today from last night's 'tear.' I am disgusted with *EVERYTHING*!!!!!

"April 7, Wed. Perry left us today; he is going to mine in Cariboo Country. I took a walk towards Esquimalt in the morning, and rode over in the afternoon. Sent letters to Louise, Jim. Truslow & to Capt. Henriques. Drew $225.-- and paid Dick $64.--

"April 8, Thur. Left Victoria at 9.30 A.M. -- Str. 'Active' left at 10, intending to beat us to Frisco. At 1:25 P.M. passed propeller 'Gussie Telfair.' At 1:30 'Active' nearly hull down. At 4 P.M. nothing to be seen of her but smoke. At 5.45 P.M. rounded Tatouche Id. Light, (Cape Flattery).

"April 9, Fri. Early in the morning we imagined we saw the smoke of the 'Active' but at 8 A.M. nothing in sight. Light breeze -- long swell. At 9 A.M. Cape Disappointment on the port beam. Stopped at 9.15 A.M. to set up an eccentric cam. From 10 A.M. to 12 M. we were surrounded by *millions* of seals, and we saw any number of whales; some of them came right alongside the ship. Passed close to an immense walrus. Light breeze. [The *Saginaw* evidently passed through the fur seal herd on its annual migration to the Pribilof Islands. The "immense walrus" was probably a big sea lion.]

"April 10, Sat. Pleasant all day; light wind; long swell. Saw more seals, whales, etc.

"April 11, Sun. Heavy N.W. wind, everything set, making about 10 knots. At sundown it came on to blow quite heavily; quite a sea on but as we are running right before the wind, we don't roll much. Off Pt. De Reyes we were obliged to haul off shore, consequently got in trough of sea. I was half asleep when I was assailed by a shower of books, pamphlets, etc., from the top of bookcase. Jumped up in time to catch some of the things in the pantry; chair upset. Sounds in the ward-room like those produced by a bull in a china store. Never saw a vessel roll so before in my life; seemed as though she *must* go clear over. Arrived at Frisco at 4 A.M. (12th).

"April 12, Mon. Got two letters from Mother, 1 from Jim Pratt and 1 from Kate. Received orders to proceed to Mare Id. where the ship will be laid up. If I don't see about 'the farm', I will have to 'klataw copa Staten Id.' The 'Active' came in at 10 A.M."

Later that year the *Active* would carry former Secretary of State William H. Seward and members of his party to Alaska.

Meigs went to Mare Island in the *Saginaw* and was present on April 17 when her flag was hauled down and she was decommissioned. The ship's final days are chronicled in Chapter 11. Commander Meade left for New York via the Overland Route on April 22. Meigs left San Francisco on April 30 aboard the *Montana* for Panama and arrived in New York on May 25.

Lieutenant Commander Richard W. Meade, Jr.

Peveril Meigs

Kitchnatti (Saginaw Jake)

Fort Wrangel, military post (photo by Muybridge)

Fort Wrangel, Indian village (photo by Muybridge)

Fort Tongass, military post (photo by Muybridge)

Fort Tongass, group of Indians (photo by Muybridge)

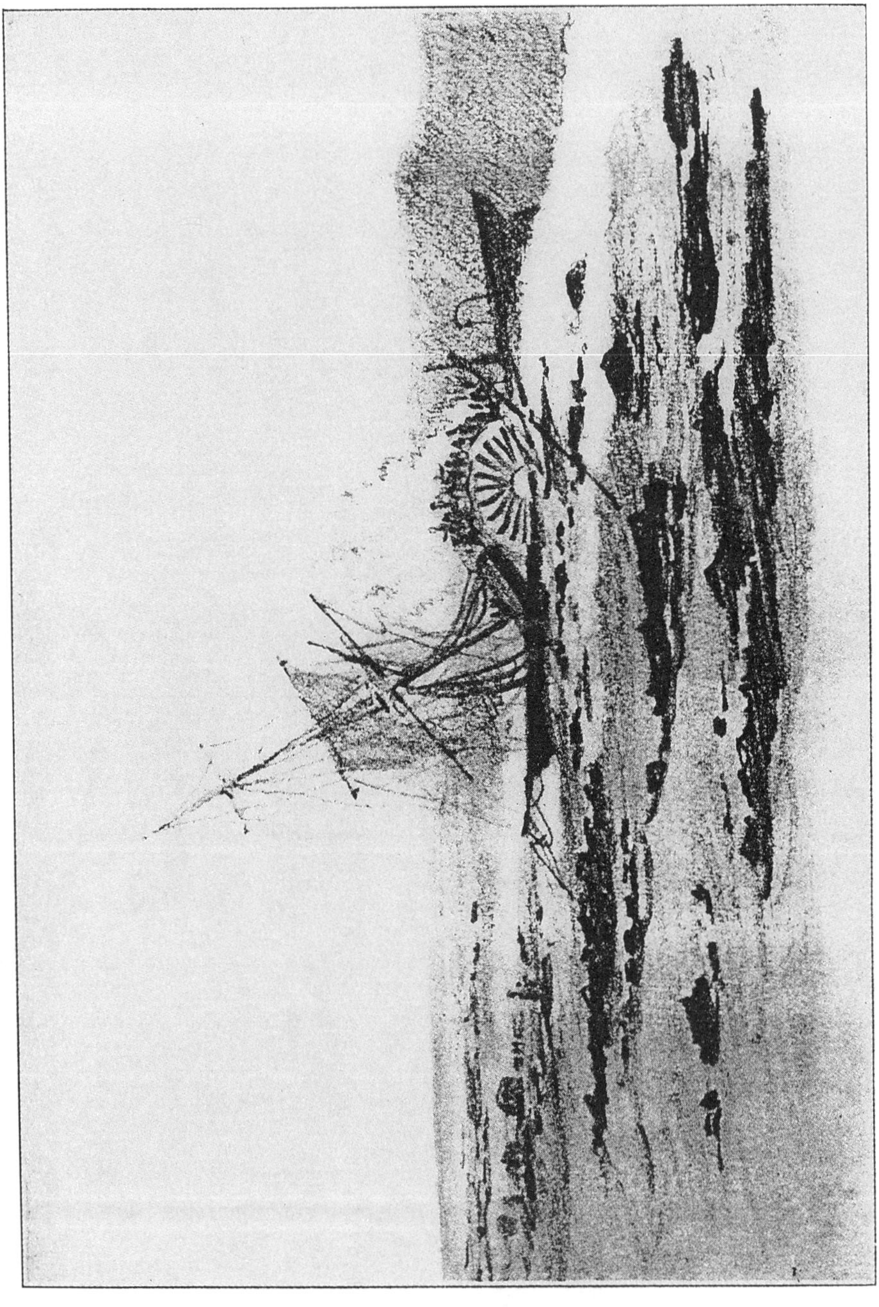

End of the *Saginaw*, November 1870

XI

EPILOGUE

THE SHIP

After being decommissioned at the Mare Island Navy Yard on April 17, 1869, the *Saginaw* was placed back in service later that year and sent back to her old patrol grounds, the west coast of Mexico. She was in charge of Lieut.-Commander Montgomery Sicard and while in southern waters members of her crew contracted yellow fever. At one time there were 25 cases on board and while there was only one death, the ship returned to San Francisco so the others could recuperate. Some repairs were made to the ship at Mare Island.

On February 22, 1870, Commander Sicard was ordered to take his ship to Midway Island, via Honolulu, as support for a contractor who was to blast a channel into the island's lagoon so it could be utilized for a coaling station. The *Saginaw* spent six days at Honolulu, refitting and taking aboard fresh stores, and arrived at Midway on March 24. During the next few months she made several trips to Honolulu for supplies, then on October 29 took on board the contractor's crew for the return to San Francisco.

Instead of heading east, however, Commander Sicard pointed his ship west toward Ocean Island, about 50 miles west of Midway. It was a tiny point of land surrounded by a coral reef and was uninhabited. Several ships had been wrecked there in the past and the exact position of the island was in dispute. Commander Sicard planned to sail around it, taking observations, and incidentally to look for shipwrecked sailors. He planned to reach the island at daylight but instead found his ship in the breakers at 3 A.M.

The *Saginaw* was soon pounded to pieces on the coral reef. All hands got ashore and managed to salvage some foodstuffs and a few other items. The ship's best boat was destroyed but the gig was carried high on the reef. Work began at once to fit her for a voyage to Honolulu, some 1,400 miles to the east. Lieut. John J. Talbot volunteered to command the gig and sailed with four men on November 18. They endured great hardships but reached Kauai Island at night just a month later. In attempting to get into a harbor they got in the breakers and capsized. Only William Halford survived and reached shore.

Halford was taken to Honolulu where he told the story of the wreck. The steamer *Kilauea*, owned by the king of the Sandwich Islands, was sent to Ocean Island. The survivors were picked up on January 3, 1871, after having spent more than two months on the desolate island.

A Court of Inquiry found that the wreck of the *Saginaw* was caused by a current that took her to the vicinity of the reef earlier than was anticipated.

The Kake War

One consequence of the destruction of the scattered Kake villages was the consolidation of all of them into a single town, on Kupreanof Island. The *Saginaw* probably hastened the amalgamation but it undoubtedly would have happened eventually without her ministrations. It was the trend among the Native villages of Southeastern Alaska.

The murders that brought on the destruction of the villages were not forgotten but nothing was done for a long time about apprehending the guilty party or parties. A Kake man named Quanni-na-qua — in the court records shortened to Quanni — was identified as the principal culprit.

At the request of Governor Swineford, the USS *Pinta* left Sitka on the day before Christmas in 1885. No emergency was apparent and the reason for that sailing day was not explained. Aboard the ship in addition to her regular crew were deputy U.S. Marshals John Hanlan and George Kostrometinoff and two members of the Indian Police force that had been started by the Navy and continued by the governors. Their names were Katlean and Dick. The mission was three-fold: To destroy as many hoochinoo stills as could be found, to free any Indian slaves that were discovered, and to arrest Quanni if he could be apprehended.

They had some success in the first two programs and complete success in the third one. The *Pinta*, after stopping at several other villages, arrived at Security Bay on January 14, 1886. Quanni was found in his home there and was arrested without a struggle. The officers were told by other villagers, however, that Quanni had not been the principal actor in the murder of Maager and Walker. The actual murderer, they said, was one of Quanni's brothers and that he was one of eight men killed in a fight the previous year. How much weight was given to that story in subsequent proceedings is difficult to determine.

When the *Pinta* returned to Sitka, Quanni was arraigned before U.S. Commissioner John G. Brady. He stated that one of his brothers had been killed at Sitka by a soldier but that when he appealed to General Davis for compensation he was repulsed and abused. The two white men were killed in retaliation, he said, but it was a family affair and only his family was responsible. He felt that the government was unfair in destroying several villages for the crime of one family. Judge Brady bound him over to the grand jury at the May term of court.

The grand jury indicted Quanni on the charge of murder and the trial was set for 10 A.M. on Saturday, May 22. Many Sitka Indians were present in the court room, according to the *Alaskan*. Before a jury could be empaneled, however, Quanni's attorney entered a demurrer to the indictment. The attorney was not named by the newspaper but probably was Willoughby Clark. A few days earlier Clark had represented the slave Sah-Quah before the court and secured his freedom. That case was reviewed by Judge James Wickersham in "Alaska

Reports." Unfortunately, the Quanni case was not reviewed in those reports and a search did not turn up a copy of the demurrer.

Judge Lafayette Dawson delayed consideration of the matter. The *Alaskan*, under its court report for May 29, said: "In U.S. vs. Quanni-na qua: Demurrer to indictment sustained and prisoner discharged with an explanation and caution."

That apparently was the end of the whole sad affair.

Commander Meade

According to one source, while Meade was in Alaska he was "occupied in surveying and keeping refractory Indians quiet."[1] After he returned to the East in April 1869 he was on "special duty" until November, then was assigned to ordnance duty and during the next nine months thoroughly inspected all of the principal gun foundries in the country. He completed that duty in July 1870 and immediately took command of the famous yacht *America* which was used as a training vessel by the Naval Academy. *America* raced in the first defense of the cup she had brought home from Britain 29 years earlier. Commander Meade did not sail her in the race and she did not win it, but she did beat the British entry, the *Cambria.*

Commander Meade next was a member of the Board to Inspect Midshipmen in the class of 1869, after which he returned to the Pacific. From February 15, 1871, until April 22 1873, he commanded the USS *Narragansett* on a 60,000-mile voyage among the islands of the Pacific. The ship had steam power as well as sails but because coaling stations were few in that area, the voyage of 60,000 miles was almost entirely under sail. Commander Meade protected American interests at several places and was commended by the Secretary of the Navy "for great judgment and skill" in negotiating a commercial treaty with the Samoan or Navigator Islands.

In May 1873 Commander Meade was assigned to special duty to prepare a report on American trade in the Pacific. Once that was completed he spent three years as

Inspector of Ordnance at the New York Navy Yard. He then commanded the *Vandalia* in the North Atlantic Squadron for three years and was made a captain on March 13, 1880. He was in charge of the Washington Navy Yard for three years, rose to the rank of commodore in 1892 and was the Navy's representative at the World Columbian Exposition at Chicago that year. While on that duty he supervised the construction of a brick replica of a battleship, one of the attractions of the fair.

After he became Rear Admiral Meade in August 1894, he was selected to command the North Atlantic Squadron. In 1895 he became dissatisfied with his relations with the Navy Department, resigned his command and voluntarily retired. He made his home at Germantown, Pennsylvania, until his death at Washington, D.C., on May 4, 1897. He was buried at Arlington National Cemetery and was survived by a son and four daughters.

Meade Point, at the entrance to Security Bay, Kuiu Island, was named for Richard Worsam Meade in the 1880s. A glacier and a river in Alaska were also named for him.

NOTE

1. Lewis R. Hamersly, *The Records of Living Officers of the U.S. Navy and Marine Corps*, 3rd. ed. (Philadelphia: J. B. Lippincott, 1878), p. 145.

APPENDIX

1.

Two letters from Lieut.-Commander John G. Mitchell, USN, to Rear Admiral Thomas T. Craven, USN, Commander-in-Chief, North Pacific Squadron, San Francisco. August 22 and 31, 1868, published courtesy of Archives, University of Alaska, Fairbanks. Collection: U.S. Navy, U.S.S. SAGINAW, Box #1.

U.S.S. "Saginaw",
Victoria V. I.,
August 22nd., 1868.

Admiral:

I respectfully request that the following with regard to Greenback pay in Alaska, may be laid before the Navy Department as an act of justice to those of the Squadron engaged in these waters.

As I understand the matter, the personnel of any vessel or vessels of the Squadron there, receive pay in Greenback because Alaska is now American soil, and, consequently its inhabitants subject to American law.

It is well worth while to know who *are* the inhabitants of Alaska.

In the first place, there is only one town or corporation, which pretends to have any civil government; and that is Sitka, the inhabitants of which exclusive of the military and the few Russians about leaving, are a few Speculators, and Jews, and the Sutlers Dept.

APPENDIX

Outside the town are the Indians, the tribe of Sitkas, about 1000 (one thousand) in number, living in all the filth and stench imaginable.

Then there are two other places, the sites of Military posts, Wrangle Island and Tungass, the latter of which does not even boast of a Sutlers shop.

The balance of the inhabitants of the territory are Indians, and some of them not particularly tame.

From these last, we, the officers at least, are obliged to purchase the greater part of our mess supplies, viz: vegetables, meats, fish etc.

The Indians do not know what paper money is. They say, on looking at it, that they can get similar papers from cans of preserved fruit, vegetables, oysters, any can, in fact.

They do understand what silver is. Suppose, however, that we purchase everything from the sutler and pay double the price in coin that *you* pay in San Francisco, selling one greenback for from 3 to 5 prct lower than the lowest quotations, which quotations may perhaps be four or five months old, at least till there is some provisional Government established, and mail communication regular.

For the time being, let Sitka be considered as being Alaska and Alaska American soil, and then let the question be put: why should those of our Squadron there receive their full pay in Greenbacks while other vessels have their *expences* in coin?

The answer can only be: you have a Sutlers store there, and the privilege of paying more than double price for the necessities of life; or additionally; you have the further privilege of being rained or snowed on for ten months out of the year, and have to purchase at advanced prices many mere articles of dry and warm clothing.

And again, you are cut off for the greater part of the time from the world, and are, in fact, as much exiles as you would be in Siberia.

Having considered the disadvantages under which the officers labor, I would like to say a few words on behalf of the crew.

They will be put to some inconvenience for warmer clothing, in purchasing which they will have to convert greenbacks, as I have already stated at a considerable discount.

When I was shipping the "Saginaws" crew in San Francisco, I was assured by Admiral Thatcher and the Fleet Paymaster that we were to have *all* Specie by authority of the Navy Department, and on this assurance I guaranteed the men shipped that they should be so paid. They shipped only on these conditions knowing our destination to be Alaska.

It was only on the eve of sailing that I was informed to the contrary.

What coin I drew here in April by Admiral Thatchers permission, I have paid out as equally as I have been able, and there is now none left.

In the home Squadron, I am informed, that whether the vessels are in or out of an American port, those on board when Paydays come, receive a certain percentage say (½) one half their monthly pay in coin. Why should we not do the same? Why should one or more vessels be deprived of a benefit, the rest of the Squadron enjoy in this particular?

Respectfully submitting the above;

I am

(Signed) John G. Mitchell
Lt. Commdr.

Rear Admiral
Thos. T. Craven U.S.N.
Comdr-in-Chief, N. Pacific Squadron, San Francisco

U.S.S. "Saginaw"
Victoria, V I,
August 31st., 1868.

Admiral:

I am still detained here by repairs on the machinery and wheels, su (sic) surveys; but it looks now as though there was some chance of leaving during the present week.

APPENDIX

The work ought to have been finished sooner, but for the great scarcity of machinists and black smiths.

I have been very impatient to get away especially since the news has reached here of the boarding and robbing of the English sch. "Black Diamond" by a party of the Hanega tribe of Indians some 80 miles from Sitka.

This is one of the (3) three tribes of Indians in the Inland waters that I have not visited. But for the "Suwanee" failing us I should have gone through them also.

I have made it a point to stop at every place where there was even a village however small on my passages to and from different points in our possessions North.

The tribes yet to be visited are the Takus, Hoonahs of Cross Sound, and the Hanegas, which will receive my immediate attention.

Until the military have some means of transportation the "Saginaw" will have to do the principal part of the work of disciplining the Indians. Thus far our presence in, and among those we have visited has been very salutary, as has been shown at Wrangle Island, Kessen, Kau Island, Koutznow and at the mouth of the Tchillcat River.

I am engaged in preparing for the information of the Department statistics of the different tribes, their chiefs, number of tribe, reliability etc; in fact everything about them which may be of interest.

The languages of them is also receiving considerable attention, as I have time to devote to them. I have a dictionary and phrase-book pretty well underweigh, of the common language spoken by all the tribes, Except the Ssimpscan to the Northward of Tungass Island, and hope to complete it during the winter.

I found it necessary to learn this one language as the tribes to the Northward of Prince Frederick sound do not understand the Chinook jargon; and in fact but few of the Indians out of the British Possessions talk the Chinook even averagely well. I have only seen two Indians North of Prince Frederick Sound that talked it at all. It seems strange that they have not learned it, for they are not at all lacking in intelligence, and the more powerful tribes are there.

APPENDIX

It would be a great advantage to us if we had a small steam tug, fitted to carry one of our (24) pds Howitzers, in case it was necessary to visit some point where it might not be expedient to move the "Saginaw". It might perhaps be cheaper in coal, although I think coal will be quite reasonable in price by Spring; perhaps as low as the Navaims (sic) coal at the mine and of a better quality.

As the mail is about closing I shall have to end this now. Hoping that its contents may be satisfactory to you,

I am etc. etc.,
(Signed) John G. Mitchell
Lt. Commander.

Rear Admiral
Thos. T. Craven U S N.
Comdg N. P. Squadron.
U.S.S. "Pensacola", San Francisco

2.

Articles by Lieut.-Commander Richard W. Meade, USN, published in *Appleton's Journal*, New York, in 1871. "Alaska" appeared in two parts. Part I, excerpts of which are given here, appeared in the July 22 issue; Part II appeared in the July 29 issue. "A Coal-Field in Alaska" was published in *Appleton's* on September 2, 1871.

ALASKA[1]

I.

Russia discovered Alaska and it remained in her possession until the 18th of October, 1867, when the blue Cross of St. Andrew, which floated over the rocky citadel at Sitka, gave place to the Stars and Strips, amid the cheering of the troops, both Russian and American, and the thundering echoes of two national salutes from the men-of-war in the harbor.

How did we come to get this vast Territory of four hundred and fifty thousand square miles, a tract of country ten times as large as the great State of New York?

Why, Mr. Seward, our late secretary of state, bought it, and Uncle Sam paid the czar seven million two hundred thousand dollars for it — a very considerable sum in these hard times, and one that an economically-disposed individual might eke out life on, if he managed his affairs well. Suppose this amount of money to be out at interest for fifty years at seven per cent, will Alaska be worth the result at the end of that time? The object of these papers is to settle that point in the mind of the reader.

The wits of the time made very merry over Governor Seward's acquisition, just as former generations of wits made merry over the acquisition of Louisiana and Florida. Mr. Seward, however, tells us that Alaska was purchased because of its natural wealth in timber, fisheries, minerals, and fur-bearing animals, and for a political object — to neutralize the power of Great Britain in the North Pacific, and render the annexation of British Columbia but a question of time.

"Alaska," said he, "may not be so valuable as we deem it; but you cannot deny the value of the gold-regions of the Cariboo country and Fraser's River, the coal-mines of Vancouver's and Queen Charlotte's Island, and the unrestricted possession of the magnificent Straits of Fuca. All these, following manifest destiny, will be ours in time. Besides," said he, "we owe a deep debt of gratitude to Russia for her unvarying friendship through long years, and for her kindly sympathy during the sorest of our national trials — the great rebellion."

Perhaps no territory of equal extent on the globe, except Central Africa, is so little known; for even now, although we have been flooded with books from travellers claiming to have explored this country, the interior is yet an unknown land. In the interior the climate is doubtless very severe, but this writer passed a winter in Alaska in 60° lat.[2] and the lowest the Fahrenheit thermometer stood at any time was 23°, while in the summer the average temperature is about 56°. Certainly not a very rigorous climate for such a latitude, and yet some may be inclined to doubt all this unless a reason is given for such an unusual temperature in such a high latitude. . . .

Well, in the Pacific Ocean there is a great current of warm water, resembling the Gulf Stream in the Atlantic, which, sweeping along the coasts of Japan and Asia, crosses the Pacific, and washes the northwest coast of America. . . .

The result of this great Pacific stream is to produce a singularly mild climate in the region under its influence, and in the northern latitudes we hear of a prevalence of much fog, while the moisture deposited upon the lofty mountains of the Alaska coast creates rain.

APPENDIX

A cold snap is a godsend at Sitka, for it is no exaggeration to say that there it rains fully two-thirds of the time. May, June, July, and February, are the driest months, and the region about Sitka may be said to be one of incessant rain-storms, fierce gales, dripping forests. dank moss, dense mud, and drifting mists. . . .

Occasionally, however, the sun does break through the damp clouds, and then, for two or three days — never longer — there is gorgeous weather. The air becomes soft and balmy, even in midwinter, when the sun rises at nine o'clock and goes down again at three, and the skies become more beautifully blue and cloudless than in any other part of the world. For two or three days there is weather calculated to make men young again, and so all Sitka turns out, including the animals, to seek the brief sunshine and bask in its transient warmth. After which the great floodgates of heaven are opened again and it is one continuous rain, rain, rain, for weeks.

Of course, in a country where it rains so constantly, the character of the crops produced on the land must be somewhat peculiar. In point of fact, though the writer of this heard a good deal of crops before he went to Alaska, he never saw any there. There were, to be sure, some watery-looking potatoes about the size of a chestnut, and some equally-miserable turnips and cabbage, but they, too, had water in them, and cabbage and water is poor diet. But certain things do grow pretty well in Alaska, among them cranberries and berries of all kinds, though they are without flavor.

ALASKA[3]

II.

TIMBER is the chief vegetable product of Alaska. The forests, which extend from Fort Tongas, on the southern boundary, to Cook's Inlet, where the trees begin to disappear, are boundless in extent, and able to supply for ages to come such countries as California and Northern Mexico, which have a poor supply of timber. There is a large and growing timber-trade carried on from Puget Sound, in Washington Territory, but the timber of Alaska, and especially the yellow cedar of Sitka, is far superior to any thing produced there. The timber is so dense in the wooded portions of Alaska, that it is difficult to make one's way any distance from the beach. Exploring parties from ships have been three and four hours getting half a mile from the beach, and, except where the timber has been cleared away for settlements, this is generally true of the whole sea-board to Cross Sound. One of the curious features of the timbered portion of this country is, that the entire surface of the ground is covered with *sphagnum*, a sort of thick, beautifully-green moss, seldom less than a foot, and sometimes even three feet deep. It forms a soft, marshy surface, into which the foot sinks at every steep; and, as it is everlastingly raining here, of course the ground is always soaking wet. If a fire is built in the woods, it is a curious sight to see it sinking down, down, until it comes to "hardpan," when you have the fire burning in a hole a foot deep or more.

Water-power for the saw-mill is every where, for the country abounds in running streams; but, even if there were none, the incessant rains would soon supply all the power needed.

Next in order, after the timber, is the fishery question, and here a word or two of preface.

The influence of a great fishery interest can hardly be over-estimated--the herring, for instance, having been described by certain enthusiasts as "a natural product whose use has decided the destiny of nations." This is putting it in rather a forcible way, and yet, without going quite so far, it is easy to see that the fisheries in the North Pacific must eventually exercise a great influence over the population, thus giving a new life to commerce, and enlarging the national resources. The fisheries are the great nurseries for seamen, who, of course, are Indispensable for commerce on the ocean. A great commerce gives power to control the sea, and "the nation which controls the sea, controls the world."

Therefore, looking at it in this light, the value of a great fishery interest in the North Pacific cannot he exaggerated, and how soon we may have one the reader can judge for himself, when he is told that there are now between fifty and one hundred vessels (many of which are New-England built and manned, and have doubled Cape Horn within the last three years) engaged in this business. And with all Mexico, Central and South America for a market — for these people must, perforce, have their Friday's fish — the business cannot fail to be a great one.

Our New-England cod and other fisheries bring us over two million dollars annually, and they are far inferior to the French fisheries in value, and still more so to the fisheries of Great Britain.

Now, of fish there is in Alaska an inexhaustible quantity, from the cod and halibut found on the banks, near Oonalaska Island and other places, to the salmon-fisheries of every fresh-water stream in the Territory, and the oolacan or candle fisheries of the Portland Channel and Naas. These last deserve especial mention. The candle-fish is not much larger than the smelt, which it much resembles in appearance, being a beautiful little fish with bright silvery skin and scales. It is caught by the Indians on bright moonlight nights. They use for this purpose a large rake some six or seven feet long, with teeth of bone or sharp-pointed nails. This rake has a handle, and, while one Indian paddles the canoe close to the "shoal of fish," the other sweeps the rake through the dense mass, bringing up generally three or four fish impaled on each tooth of the rake. The canoes are soon filled, and, the contents being taken on shore, the squaws proceed to skewer the fish on long stick , passing these stick through the eyes until each one has as many as it will hold, when the whole are suspended in the thick, smoky atmosphere at the top of the hut, which dries and preserves the fish without salt, which is never used by the Indians.

When dry, the candle-fish are carefully packed away in boxes of dried hark. The traders at Fort Simpson catch these fish in nets, salt and dry them in the usual manner practised by the whites, and, when this is properly done, no fish are more delicious than the candle-fish, the only trouble being that they are so rich one soon tires of them.

To use them as candles, a piece of wick, or dried pith, is passed through the fish with a bodkin of hard wood, and the tail being inserted in a cleft-stick, or junk-bottle, the wick is lighted. The fish burns with a clear, steady flame.

Of salmon there are myriads. Every fresh-water stream is filled with them during the season, which commences in the latter part of June. At that period the Indians lay in their winter's supply of food, by selecting some fresh-water stream about forty feet wide, which has a slight fall of water, say six feet or so, a short distance from where it empties into the sea. Above the fall they either stretch a net or make a weir of twigs and stakes entirely across the stream. When the salmon commence "to run," as the saying is, they make for the streams, and go with a jump clear over the fall into the net, and are scooped out or struck with spears, and thus landed on the river-bank, where they are dried on poles stretched across a frame. The first "run" has the choice fish.

At the bay of Cossan is a salmon-fishery owned by a Russian named Baronovitch. He informed the writer of this article that he had seen the fish so thick in the streams as to impede a canoe, and the same story has been told elsewhere. Baranovitch, with limited means, puts up about one thousand barrels of fish every season, and could put up ten times that number if he had the capital. In Alaska salmon is a drug on the market, and, throughout the length and breadth of the Territory a white man will not touch it if he can get any thing else; but what the Indian would do without it is hard to say; it is his staple of food — he could not exist without it.

Timber and fish having been disposed of, next in order are the furs.

Prior to our acquisition of the country the trade in furs was in the hands of two great corporations, the Russian-

American Fur Company and the Hudson Bay Company, the latter having leased certain locations, and obtained certain rights from the former.

The Hudson Bay Company is much the older of the two, and its original members in 1670, when it was first chartered by the British crown, were such noted characters in history as Prince Rupert, the Duke of Albermarle and the Earl of Craven. It maintained many ships, and grew rich and powerful by its trade. Its profit in furs was enormous, so much so that half the stories told by the veterans in the trade seem hardly credible. One is to the effect that, a few years ago, the price of a flint-lock musket in furs was found by standing the musket on its butt-end and piling up marten-furs until they reached the muzzle. Now, these muskets never cost the company over two dollars a piece, and thus several hundred marten-skins, worth from three to thirty dollars a piece, were obtained for a mere song!

But these golden days have passed and gone forever, and the natives know the full value of their furs now.

One may, therefore, gather an idea — a faint one — of the enormous profits formerly realized in this business. The most valuable of all the furs is the sea-otter, which now brings from twenty-five to seventy-five dollars *in Alaska.* It is a beautifully soft purplish-black fur and very heavy, and in Russia is known as the "court fur," only to be worn by certain classes of the nobility. For any plebeian to wear this fur in Russia is an offence punished by fine, imprisonment or exile to Siberia.

The fur is also extensively sought after by the higher classes in the Chinese empire, hence its very high price. The animal is now scarce, and only to be taken among the Aleutian Islands, the noise of fire-arms having driven it from the Alexander Archipelago.

After the sea-otter, in point of importance to the trader, are the black and silver foxes, also very valuable; then come the furred seal, marten, or Hudson Bay sable, crossed fox, mink, ermine, and red fox; after which come such inferior furs as the hear, lynx, wolverine, mountain-sheep, and many others, the number of fur-bearing animals being very great.

Of all these animals the furred seal is the one most likely to prove valuable for revenue. It is found almost solely on the islands of St. Paul and St. George, to the north of the Aleutian chain, hence known as the Seal Islands, though late accounts now say it resorts to the Commander group. It is different from the common seal, and is one of the most sagacious and intelligent of dumb creatures — in fact, its instinct is almost human. The nervous organization of the animal is peculiar, and so sensitive is he to sharp sounds and noises that the firing of guns or barking of small dogs will cause them to desert their usual haunts, and the keeping of a little dog on St. Paul's Island during a certain year is said to have caused the Russian Fur Company a loss of over one hundred thousand dollars' worth of furs the next year. Consequently, an indiscriminate free trade in these animals would soon cause them to desert the islands now resorted to altogether, and, therefore, a monopoly of this business is essential to its life. Indiscriminate butchery of the seal would also soon glut the market and lower the price so as hardly to pay for transportation. The Russians only allowed a certain number (about eighty thousand) to be killed annually, and this kept the price up, and the seal were not reduced in numbers.

When the season arrives (between May and October), these animals flock to the islands mentioned in incredible numbers and with an organization and system truly wonderful. In one division of a herd are the females with their young; in another division, the young males and females, separated; while the old males preserve order throughout the herd, and act as overseers, constables, and whippers-in generally. If a young male gets in among the females, away goes one of these old chaps for him, and drives him back again with his tail. They have never been known to have any thing resembling the Sorosis among them.

On the arrival of the herd the natives select certain of them for slaughter, quietly drive them into the interior of the island away from the main body, where they are killed with a blow on the nose from a club, the skin stripped off and salted down, and the flesh used to make oil and for many other purposes. The young males and females are the ones selected for slaughter, which is the appreciation the natives set on single blessedness.

The furs when first taken are coarse and have to be sent to Europe to be prepared for the market. In England they are frequently dyed afterward.

But the fur-trade generally throughout the Alexander Archipelago is likely, under the present system, or rather want of system, to die out altogether, since, in course of time, the wholesale slaughter of fur-bearing animals will exterminate them. Under the Russian monopoly the animals were not only protected by statute but in fact, and the natives were not allowed to kill them indiscriminately. This prevented the stock from becoming extinct, and kept the price of furs up. But with all its power — the power of life and death — the company could not prevent an illicit trade in furs carried on by the English and American whiskey-smugglers from British Columbia and Washington Territory. These scoundrels plied the Indians with liquor of the vilest description, and took their furs from them in exchange.

As a specimen of the manner in which this is done, it may here be mentioned that, in 1868, a fellow named Coffin sailed in a schooner from a port int British Columbia with a cargo of villainously bad alcohol and some common sugar. Of course, water costs nothing in this country, and so Captain Coffin was enabled to manufacture a drink which would veritably take a man's scalp off at forty rods!

But he knew how to tickle the palate of the Indian, who judges of liquor solely by its fiery taste, and values it in proportion to the amount it takes to produce intoxication — a "cheap drunk" being a great thing in Alaska.

This fellow, by the sale of his infamous decoction, brought on difficulty between two tribes of Indians before friendly to each other, and seventeen of the Hudson Bay Indians were killed in a fight which subsequently ensued. But he and his vessel shortly after came to grief, being wrecked on Forrester's Island, and Coffin and his companions were found on the beach dead, with their throats so torn and lacerated that for a long time it was though they had been murdered by the Indians. Subsequently it was ascertained that the sharp rocks on the beach were responsible for the mutilated condition of the bodies.

Of course, if the fur-trade is to fall into the hands of such fellows as Coffin in a few years it will be conducted on the whiskey basis unless the United States Government takes the most rigid and inflexible means to suppress it.

The natives themselves give aid and comfort to the whiskey-smuggler by timely warning of approaching danger, by false information to the officers of the law, and by secreting the small vessels of these smugglers when searched fur. The myriads of islands and harbors along this coast, which resembles Norway in the character of its fiords; the thick, foggy weather, and the innumerable channels and straits, many of which are not even marked on the charts, give an advantage to the whiskey-trader he is not slow to avail himself of.

Lastly, among the supposed resources of the country is its mineral wealth, and, in regard to this, not much is actually known, for, under the rule of the Russian Fur Company, its employee's were so busy in getting furs, and studying the best method of keeping up the supply, that no good mineralogical collection of specimens was made for comparison; while, since the country came into our possession, no regularly-organized expedition for exploration has been sent to Alaska, and the only knowledge we possess is derived from the Indians (generally unreliable), the wandering bands of prospectors, and an occasional account of an excursion from some military post. Yet gold has been discovered on the Stachine River, and the mines have been worked to some extent. Miners from there say that, with ordinary panning, they can make from two to seven dollars per day; but the pleasant season lasts only six months — the rest of the year the weather is too inclement to work in, and the isolated position of the placers renders it difficult to get provisions and stores.

Copper is said to have been discovered on the Copper River, and there is no doubt but that copper utensils were in use among the natives as far back as the days of Behring, though where the copper cane from the historian sayeth not.

Silver, iron, and bismuth are said to exist, but the writer of this never saw any one in Alaska who could testify having seen any; and as for diamonds, why, there are quantities — in New York — and sold by the veritable "Original Jacobs!" — so that the mineral wealth of the Territory is uncertain, coal being the only product in that line found there that admits of any discussion as to its probable value. In regard to coal, there is an inexhaustible supply both on Admiralty Island and at Cook's Inlet.

But nothing, as yet, has been said of the scenery — the history, climate, inhabitants, and resources of the country have all been discussed, the useful dwelt upon, the beautiful alone omitted.

Well, the traveller from Alaska may enlarge a good deal on scenery, especially when he can talk of mountain-ranges covered with perpetual snow, huge glaciers awing into silence every beholder with their magnificent sublimity, water-falls, rapid currents, and splendid forests of timber, with the Aurora Borealis thrown in every clear night by way of a make-weight.

The writer of this has no more of the romantic in him than Mark Twain, yet he can say with truth that in twenty-five years' roaming in all quarters of the globe he never saw more magnificent scenery anywhere than in British Columbia and Alaska — the only trouble is, is so continuously magnificent, it becomes monotonous.

Now let us see if it is possible to convey a faint idea of the voyage through the inland waters from Victoria, in Vancouver's Island, to Sitka, in Alaska, by means of a simile.

APPENDIX

Let us suppose the Highlands of the Hudson River (with which nearly all are familiar) to be stretched out, as it were, for nine hundred miles. We won't widen the river at all, but we will increase the height of the hills from fourteen hundred to three thousand, seven thousand, and some cases ten thousand feet. We will cover the peaks of the peaks of the mountains with snow, and the rest with dense forests of timber, except where the mountain-streams come tumbling down in great water-falls of fifty feet or more, and frequently fall over a huge cliff directly into the sea, near which our vessel passes. As we go farther north, imagine great valleys filled with enormous glaciers, or sheets of ice, from one to ten miles wide, and extending back miles into the interior. These huge masses of ice, sometimes twelve hundred feet thick, are of a blue Alpine hue, and, when the bright sunlight falls upon them, their gleaming surface, rich with prismatic color, presents an inconceivably magnificent sight.

Now, if the reader can gather any thing from this imperfect description, he has in his mind's eye the scenery of Alaska. For miles and miles our steamer journeys along through this wilderness, amid these mountains "wooded to the peak." From base to snowy region, nothing mars the uniformity — a dense, dark forest of pines and hemlock, through whose wilds the foot even of the savage has never wandered! The eye fairly wearies of the endless monotony and death-like stillness of these primeval forests, and seeks for more peaceful landscapes; but in vain. Nothing disturbs the dreary loneliness of this wonderful forest-land, except the splash of the paddles, as the steamer speeds swiftly on her way; the shrill note of the eagle, as he circles over some lofty cliff, or the howl of the wolf amid the recesses of the forest.

Everywhere the depth of water is great — two hundred fathoms of line find no bottom. The hundreds of straits and channels help to bewilder the navigator, so that it is difficult for him to grope his way through the endless labyrinth. Grenville Channel is forty-eight miles long, about a mile wide, is perfectly straight, and has but two anchorages.

On one occasion an English man-of-war lost her way in one of the "*cul-de-sac* channels," near Bella-Bella, and was nearly two weeks finding her way back again. As there is only an occasional anchorage here and there, such a predicament is exceedingly unpleasant, not say hazardous. The line of channel through this myriad of islands is rarely wider than the Hudson at Haverstraw, and is frequently not over a mile, while in some places it is hardly that; and here, through these fearful gorges, less than a mile wide, the tide runs with a terrible rapidity, to which our current of Hell Gate, near New York, is a "mere circumstance."

Imagine such a pass between ranges of lofty mountains, from three thousand to five thousand feet in height, the tide rushing through at the rate of twelve knots an hour, and the reader has some idea of the Yaculta Rapids, at Seymour Narrows, in British Columbia, and Peril Straits, in Alaska.

Several large vessels have attempted these rapids in their strength, and some have only by good fortune escaped destruction with all on board.

At this stage, I hear some reader exclaim that nothing has been said about Sitka and the Russians.

Well, Sitka may be briefly described as the dirtiest collection of log-huts on the Pacific slope. Its appearance as a town is far from inviting, and, with the magnificent scenery in the background, its squalor is all the more striking. There is an old saying that "God made the country, and man the town" — it is strikingly exemplified at Sitka.

On the right of the town, looking at it from the anchorage, stand the buildings formerly belong to the fur company, the citadel being on the rocky eminence once before spoken of; further on, the houses of the citizens; finally, the church and hospital. On the left of the town, outside of the stockade, is the Indian village of about sixty houses; still farther to the left, a collection of Indian graves.

The Russian governor's house, or the citadel, now occupied by the commanding officer of the military district, is the only building in Sitka, except the church, that deserves any especial mention. It is perched on Katlian's Rock before mentioned, and is a huge structure of two stories in height, but very long and broad, roofed with sheet iron, painted red, and capped by the only light-house in Alaska, which, at night, casts a feeble glimmer three or four miles seaward.

The summit of the hill is defended by batteries which command every point in the harbor. The northwest end is approached by a flight of wooden steps, and halfway up sentinels are kept posted day and night; at this point is a sort of military prison, in front of which is displayed a light battery of brass cannon, loaded with canister, and ready for any emergency.

The upper story of the building is divided into one large room in the centre, flanked by drawing-room and billiard-room at one end, and another large room at the other, all well kept, painted in nice style, and hung with old prints of celebrated English sea-fights. The lower story contains dining-room, parlor, study, and sleeping-apartments, all very large and furnished with the inevitable Russian stove, or furnace. The entire structure is built of huge logs, squared, joined, and painted.

There is really but one decent street in the town, to which Americans have given the title of Broadway, and, after passing the church and hospital, the street forms itself into a road along the beach, after following which for about half a mile, you reach the only natural curiosity in Sitka — a huge stone on which old Baranoff, the first governor, used to sit on fine afternoons and drink brandy until he became so much "overcome" that his friends had to take him home.

The Russians kept their houses in a filthy condition, some even kept poultry in the rooms over the sleeping-chamber, and, as the little windows were never opened except at long intervals, the odor was not exactly *bouquet de mille fleurs*. And the pigs and goats roamed the streets with unrestricted liberty.

Fortunately, most of the Russians have gone home, or to the Amoor River, and probably, aided by the everlasting rains, Sitka may eventually become clean, and the high board-walks, rendered indispensable in order to keep people out of the deep mud, be finally dispensed with.

The officers of the garrison have a club-house near the church, where, after the manner of frontier posts, they play cards and billiards, and drink commissary whiskey; that is, when the rest of their time is not taken up in lounging in the sutler's store.

The Greek church is a gaudily-decorated affair, painted in green and gold, after the Eastern fashion, with magnificent regalia and appointments for its exceedingly imposing, but rather tiresome services.

In the church was kept a magnificent Bible, presented by the czar, with jewelled cover, said to be worth a fabulous amount, and the progress of American civilization and republican institutions was marked by its being stolen upon the occupation by the Yankees.

The Indians are never allowed inside the stockade after nightfall, while a guard is kept constantly on the alert with rifles loaded, and a field-battery of Parrott guns kept constantly trained on the Indian village adjoining the town, and a man-of-war lies anchored in the harbor, with her guns pointed at the Sitka village.

The population is about fifteen hundred during the winter season, of whom one thousand are Indians, and the rest Jews, Gentiles, hickory Christians, and soldiers.

And this is the principal, and, if we except Kodiak (for Forts Tongas and Wrangel are only military posts), the only town or place of any importance in the whole Territory of four hundred and fifty thousand square miles.

And now, if the reader has had the patience and followed us attentively in this sketch, he can draw his own conclusions as to the present and prospective value of

Alaska, and whether, on the whole, it is or is not worth the money we paid for it.

RICHARD W. MEADE.

A COAL-FIELD IN ALASKA[4]

In the summer of 1868, the commander of the United States steamer Saginaw, cruising on the coast of Alaska, learned from the Indians of the existence of coal of a superior quality at Kootznahoo, on Admiralty Island. He visited the place, verified the reports of the existence of a coal resembling cannel, and brought away a considerable quantity. No survey was made, however, and, in the mean time, the vessel was ordered back to San Francisco, and the officers and crew changed. In the winter of the same year the Saginaw was again ordered to Alaska, and, upon her arrival at Sitka, found her stock of fuel reduced to twenty-six tons, while the Government supply usually kept at Sitka was utterly exhausted. To cruise in these waters in a paddle-wheel steamer without coal was impossible, and the Jews of Sitka, taking advantage of the necessities of the Government, raised the price of their coal to thirty dollars per ton, when the commander of the vessel very promptly refused to purchase. A trip to Kootznahoo was determined upon, though there was no one on board who had any knowledge of the route, and it was considered at any time a hazardous experiment, as the channel to the mine was represented to be full of sunken rocks and rapids; while, should the Saginaw run short of fuel while there, and get none to replace what she burned in getting there, she would be in rather an unpleasant predicament.

Nevertheless, a large scow to contain coal was borrowed from the quartermaster of the port, and the Saginaw left Sitka, January 13, 1869, and after a short run of sixty miles, anchored behind a small island, known to the

Indians as Kenasnow, and within two miles of the Indian village of Kootznahoo.

A few days were necessarily spent in holding a "pow-wow" with the Indians, procuring a guide, and exploring the channel leading to the coal-mines by means of the boats. The only chart in the vessel represented what is now called Kootznahoo Archipelago by a sprawling figure — a mere outline without even a name. The annexed map [not included] shows the character of the work subsequently done by the officers of the vessel, and, though not strictly accurate, is a good preliminary to any future survey.

The 17th of January was the day selected to make the trip to the mine. Slack water was chosen, and the voyage successfully accomplished through an exceedingly dangerous channel. At dusk, which in January in this latitude (57°29′ N.) occurs about three P.M., the vessel was safely anchored in a beautiful bay in the interior of the island, which, in memory of the first American officer who visited this strange region, received the name of Mitchell's Bay. An idea may be formed of the wonderful mildness of the climate, by stating that the Fahrenheit thermometer registered 41°.

The next day proved a busy one. The lighter was towed to the mine, all of the boats sent off to explore the country, and a large gang of Indians hired to dig coal and cut wood. Very soon the wilderness seemed alive with bustle and activity, and the sharp rifle-crack of the sportsmen mingled with the sound of the axe and dull thud of the pick. The surrounding country showed coal-croppings in almost every direction, though the veins seemed better in the vicinity of the lowland and on the margin of the bayous, which seemed to ramify in endless directions.

The weather being clear and mild, and the Indians working most amiably with the sailors from the vessel, so well was the labor rewarded that, in a few days, enough coal and wood was taken on board to enable the steamer to cruise for some weeks; while the actual cost of obtaining fuel proved so trifling, that the vessel was subsequently run, at a speed averaging seven knots, for the very insignificant cost of twelve dollars per day.

The Kootznahoo coal is of a recent geological formation, and resembles somewhat the cannel. The surface-coal is filled with strata of pure resin, clear as amber; some of the blocks were beautiful specimens, and it is highly inflammable, burning with a clear flame in the light of a candle.

These coal-fields seem to lie in an extensive valley between two ranges of lofty mountains. This valley is a basin, as it were, filled with innumerable islands, and its extent seems to be about fifteen miles north-northwest and south-southeast, with an average width of about five miles. The islands are small, low, and, near their borders, somewhat marshy. The entire valley is doubtless a vast coal-field.

There are two routes from Sitka to the coal-region: one by the way of Peril Straits, a narrow arms of the sea, separating Baranoff Island (upon which Sitka stands) from Tchitchagoff Island, a large island to the north; and the second out seaward, and to the southward round Cape Ommaney, and so through Chatham Straits, north again to the coal-region. The latter is preferable for large vessels, as Peril Straits are dangerous for any but steamers under fifteen feet draught, owing to the rapidity of the currents, and the numberless rocks in the channel.

Notes

[1.] *Appleton's Journal*, New York, v. 6, July 22, 1871.

[2.] This figure, coming from a Navy officer, is somewhat astonishing and especially in view of the fact that in his previous article, on the Kootznahoo coal mine, Meade gave an accurate latitude for that place. In his four months in Alaska, from December 1868 through March 1869, Meade did not get much above 59 degrees, and that only for three days. Much of his time was spent at Sitka, 57°03′ N., and Kootznahoo, at 57°29′

N. And as he was in Alaska only during the winter, much of what he wrote had to be hearsay.

[3.] *Appleton's Journal*, New York, v. 6, July 29, 1871.

[4.] *Appleton's Journal*, New York, v. 6, Sept. 2, 1871, p. 266.

3.
Chinook Language

Nika	I
Mika	You
Klasker	They
Mesika	You (pl.)
Nesika	We
Yaka	He or She
Tenass man	Boy
Chaco	Come
Momook	Work
Klatawa	Go
Kar	Where
Yawa	Here
Alta	At present
Alke	Afterwards
Illihe	Land
Hyack	Quick
Siya	Distance
Klackster	Who
Klosh	Good
Laport	Door
Konaway	All
Sun	Day
Poolakly	Night
Tenas sun	Morning
Sitkum sun	Moon
Kock wa	The same
Toolkut	Song
Hy you	Plenty
Hyas	Large
Socally	High
Pilton	Fool
Tekhope	White
Pil	Red
Klayl	Black
La tate	Head
La boosh	Mouth
La da	Teethe
Le Lang	Tongue
Seeah house	Face
La ma	Hand
Yaksoot	Hair
La reh	Barley
La peah	Peas
Wapito	Potatoes
La novow	Turnips
La karrot	Carrots
La onion	Onions
Cabbage	Cabbage
Klapite	Thread
Moola	Sawmill
Percise	Blanket
Kamoosac	Beads
Poolally	Powder
Kulla-kulla	Birds
Musket	Gun
Ninamox	Otter
Ena	Beaver
Quanice	Whale
Yuiceco	Porpoise
Oluck	Snake
Soolec	Mouse
Skad	Mole
La loe	Wolf
Pish-pish	Cat
Kuitan	Horse
Moos-moos	Cow
La mouto	Sheep
Carmox	Dog
Kushaw	Hog
Kimta	Behind
Shetsham	Swim
Seeapoose	Cap
La shawl	Shawl
Pe	And
Wechat	Also
Dly tupso	Hay
Dly	Dry
Tum-tum	Heart
Comb	Comb
Koory	Run
Pil-pil	Blood
Les eff	Egg
La pole	Hen
La chuck	Rooster
La pell	Shovel

APPENDIX

La push	Hoe	Musatchy	Bad
La clew	Nail	Tyhee	Chief
Lake	Lake	Elitee	Slave
La chaise	Chair	Ou	Brother
Kettle	Pot	Ats	Sister
Oskan	Cup	Kapswalla	Steal
Lope	Rope	Ipsoot	Secret
Silux	Angry	Potlach	Give
Shanty	Sing	Iscum	Take
Marcie	Thanks	Wake	No
Kinoose	Tobacco	Nowitka	Yes
Chee	New	Pechuck	Green
Sunday	Sunday	Lemoro	Wild
Pooh	Shoot	La selle	Saddle
Lolo	To carry	Sitlii	Stirrup
Klawa	Slow	La sibro	Spurs
Wagh	To spill	Kolan	Ear
Inti	Across	Klapp	To find
La prate	Priest	Kull	Tough-hard
La yob	Devil	Sapalel	Flour or wheat
Kapo	Relation	Pire sapalel	Bread
La pied	Foot	La bisquit	Biscuit
Tee-owitt	Leg	La ween	Oats
Yachoot	Belly	Lice	Rice
Spose	If	Sagwa	Sugar
Delate	Truth or Straight	Soap	Soap
Seepy	Crooked	Molass	Molasses
Tolo	Win	Stick-shoes	Shoes
Kow	Tie	Skin-shoes	Moccasins
Klack	Untie	Gleece pire	Candle
Man	Man	Skullapen	Rifle
Klootchman	Woman	Memoloose	Kill
Lum	Run	Actshot	Bear
Patle	Full	Mowitch	Deer
Patlamb	Drunk	Cuitchady	Rabbit
Bostan	American	Skubbyyou	Skunk
Pesioux	French	Olikhiyou	Seal
King George	English, Scotch, Irish	Yakolla	Eagle
Chuck	Water	Waugh-waugh	Owl
Oihe	Sandwich Islander	Skakairk	Hawk
Halo	None	Mauk	Duck

APPENDIX

Smock-smock	Grouse
Malaekua	Mosquito
Swaawa	Panther
Skuzdzo	Squirrel
Enpooy	Lice
La sway	Silk
Lalopa or coat	Coat
Sickilox	Pantaloons
Shirt	Shirt
Aekik	Fishhook
Tootosh	Milk
Snass	Rain
Pithick	Think
Snow	Snow
La hache	Axe
La leem	Fire
Opsu	Knife
La kley	Key
Pillom	Broom
Lakutchee	Clams
Dacassett	Trunk
Tumolitch	Barrel
Opkan	Basket
La pla	Plate
La table	Table
La geen	Saw
Moosum	Sleep
Cold illihe	Winter
Warm illihe	Summer
Cold	Year
Ke-waap	Hole
Zum	Write
Klemenwhit	False
Klonass	Doubtful, don't know
Quass	Fear, afraid
Olally	Berries
Tzae	Sweet
Tumallow	Tomorrow

Hee-hee	Laugh
Moon	Moon, Month
Klukuce	Stars
How	Listen, attend
Sil-sil	Buttons
La peep	Pipe
Akaepoi	Needle
Tin-tin	Music
Dance	Dance
Opootch	Tail
Etlinwill	Ribs
Ikt-stick	Yard
Elp	First
Klayl stone	Coal
La sack	Bag
Newha	How is it?
Tenass klootchman	Girl
Tenass	Child, anything small
Wa-wa	Language, to speak
Mamook chaco	Bring
Muck muck	Anything good to eat
Pire chuck	Ardent spirits
La plosh	Shingle or plank
Wake nika kumtox	I don't understand
Ayas	Large or very large
Till	Heavy or tired
Lazy	Slow or lazy

APPENDIX

Mammock ipsot	To conceal
Halluck la port	Open the door
Ech poy la port	Shut the door
Midlight	Sit down, put down or stay
Midwhit	Stand up, get up or move
Sitkum	Middle or half
Tenas poolakly	Sunset or dusk
Cockshut	Fight, break, injure
Wake skokum	Weak
Wake konsick	Never
Kumtux	Understand
Tikke	Want, desire
Ikta mika tikke	What do you want?
Okoak	This or that
Wake ikta nika tikke	I do not want anything
Siwash	Indian, savage
Ankuty	Long ago
Lay-lay	A long time
Konsick	How much
Makook	Buy or sell
Kultis	Nothing or gratis
Kopet	Finish or stop
Kopet wawa	Hold your tongue
Nanitch	Look, to see
Sockally tyhee	The Almighty
Keekwooly	Deep, beneath
Quonisum	Always
Sick	Sick, ill
La crem	Cream color
Leky	Spotted or piebald
Olo	Hungry or thirsty
La pushmo	Saddle blanket
Chick-chick	Wagon or car
Kull-kull stick	Oak
La plash stick	Cedar
La gum stick	Pine
Keleman sapalel	Flour
Sale	Cotton or calico
Kanim	Canoe or boat
Klackan	Fence, a field
Kalidon	Lead or shot
Chickaman	Money, and metals of all kinds
Tenass musket	Pistol
Moolack or moose	Elk
Salmon or sallo wack	Salmon

APPENDIX

Tenass salmon	Trout	Iloman	An old or worn out man
Le mule or Hyass kolon	Mule	Lemael	An old woman
Man moos-moos	Ox	Hyas Sunday	X'mas and July 4th
Henkerchiem	Handkerchief	Pisheck	Bad, exhausted
Coat	A woman's gown	Paper	Paper, books, etc
Keekwully coat	Petticoat	Zum seeahhoose	Paint the face
Keekwully sickilox	Drawers	Pire ololly	Ripe berries
Hachr or house	House	Cold ololly	Cranberries
Kata	Why or what is the matter	Fiil ololly	Strawberries
Whaah	Indeed (exclamation of astonishment)	Mapiaege	A trap or snare
Abba	Well then, if that is the case	Miami	Down the stream, below
Kuckwulla	Nut	Machlay	Toward the land
Tupso	Grass or straw	Alloyma	Another or different
Hoey-hoey	Exchange	Hee-hee la ma	Gamble
Tootosh gleece	Butter	Killapie	Return, capsize
Glass	Looking or window glass	Kloch-kloch	Oysters
Koory kuitan	Race horse	Lawoolitch	Bottle
Tenass lakutchee	Mussels	Annah	Exclamation of astonishment
Koppo	From, towards, etc.	Staetijay	Island
Chitch	Grandmother	Sick tum-tum	Regret, sorrow
		Kooy-kooy	Finger rings

APPENDIX

Hrowlkult	Stubborn, determined
Tickaerchy	Although
Temanawas	Witchcraft
Owayhee	Trail or road
Iht	1
Mox	2
Klone	3
Locket	4
Quinam	5
Tahum	6
Sinamox	7
Sootkin	8
Quies	9
Totilum	10
Totilum pe ikt	11
Totilum pe mox	12
Ikt tokamonak	100
Ikt hyas tokamonak	1,000
Stowbelow	North
Steg waak	South
Sun chacko	East
Sun midlight	West

Chaco six, nika tikke waw waw copa mika.	Come here, friend, I want to talk to you.
Nika tikke makook kanim pe locket issic.	I want to buy a canoe with four paddles.
Closhe.	Very good.
Konsick dollar nika tikke?	What is your price?
Klone totilum dollar.	Thirty dollars.
Wake six, nika marsh copa mika mox totilum dollar.	No sir, I'll give you twenty dollars.

APPENDIX

Klonass, nika nanitch.	I don't know. I'll see.
Spose nesika tikke kanim pe klatawa siya copa memoloose mowitch.	Suppose we take the canoe and go and get a deer.
Nika tum-tum mika hiu kultus waw waw.	I think you speak too much for nothing.
Mika klapp klone alloyma siwashe pe klattawa copa nesika mammook kanim sockally Fraser River copa gold ilahe?	Will you find three more Indians and go with us to work canoe up Fraser River to the gold land?
Nowitka, coqua nika tum-tum spose mika marsh hiu chickamen.	Yes, that is my mind, if you pay plenty money!

Siwash Language

Claque	1
Ta-akke	2
Nuske	3
Tar-qúne	4
Ca-chin	5
Cla-tu-shu	6
Tar-ka-tu-	7
shu	8
Nuske-tu-	9
shu	10
Cour-schuck	
Chinnekarte	

MAP No. 1.

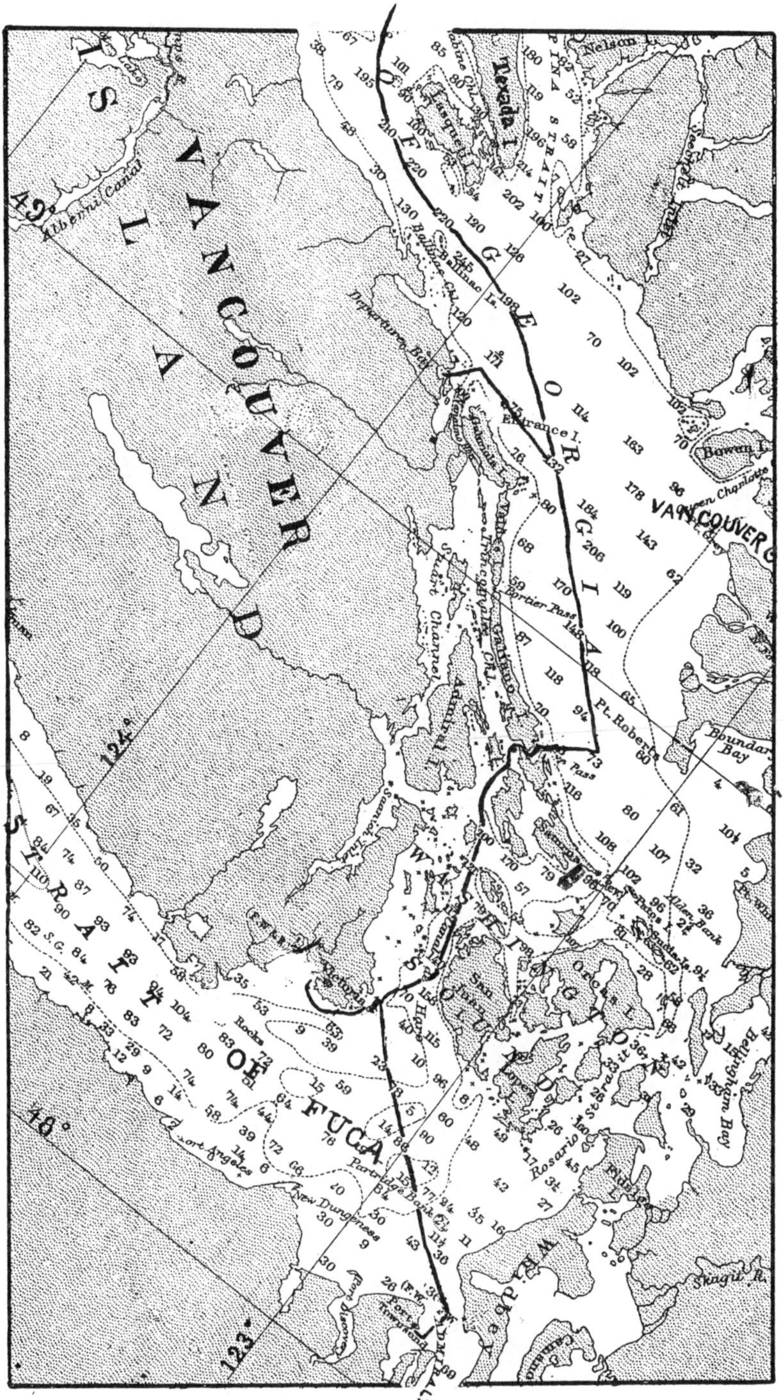

From Port Townsend to Texada Island.

MAP No. 2.

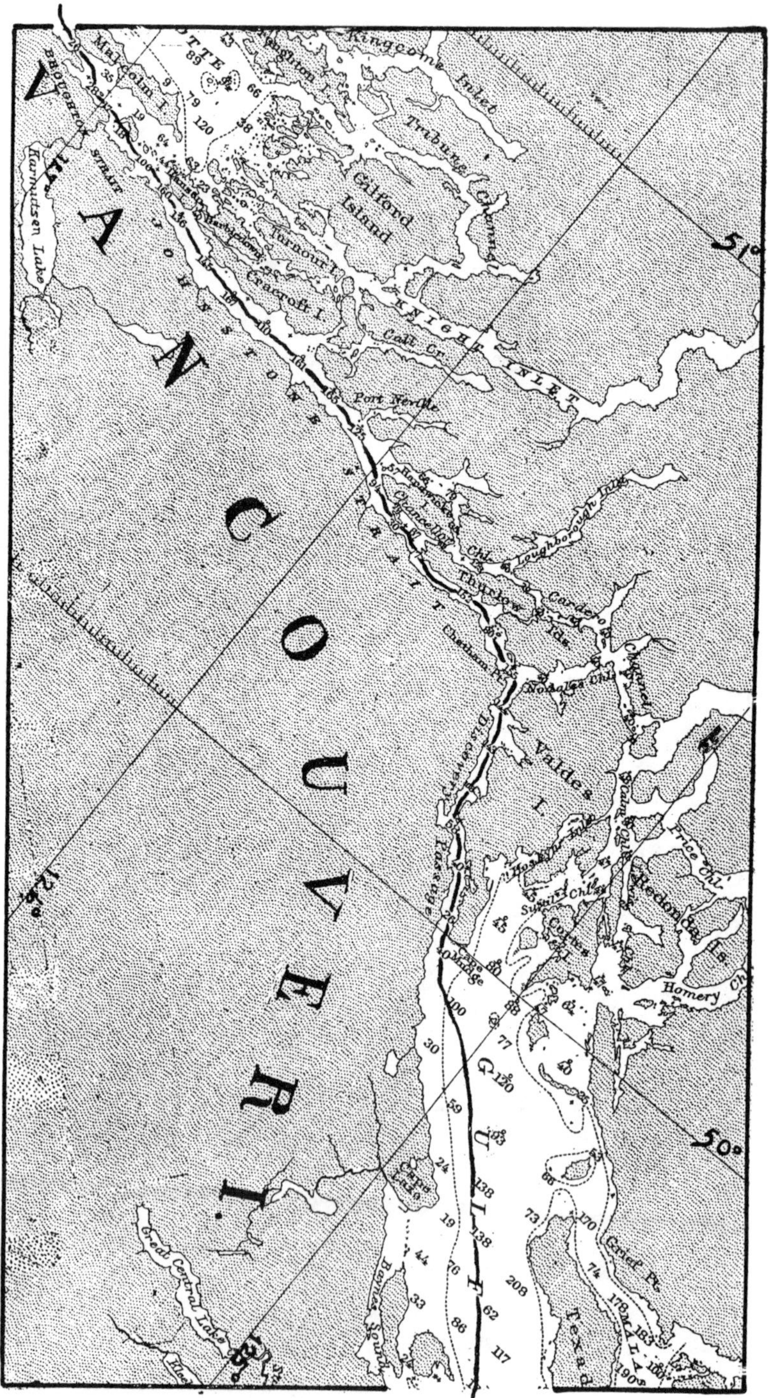

From Texada Island to Queen Charlotte Sound.

MAP No. 3.

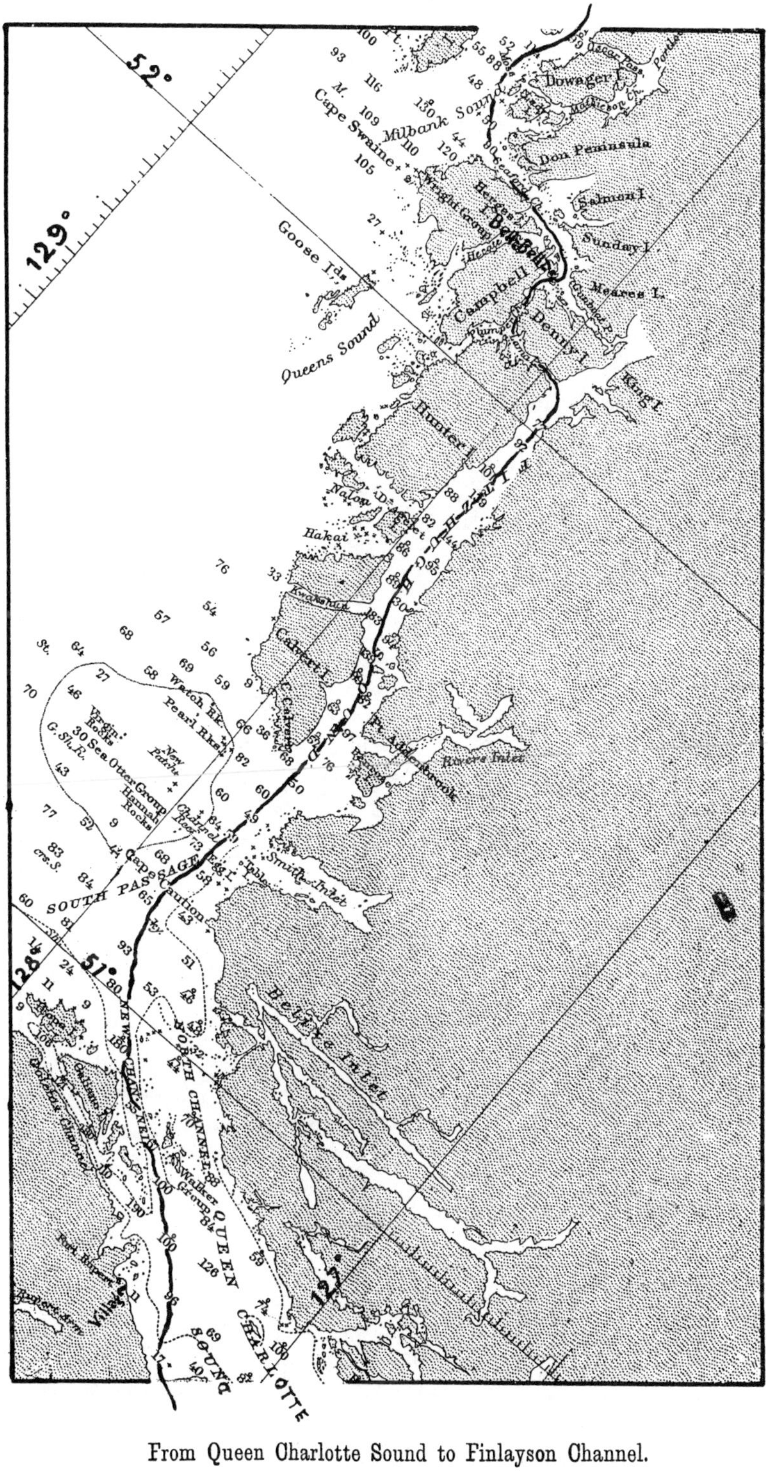

From Queen Charlotte Sound to Finlayson Channel.

MAP No. 4.

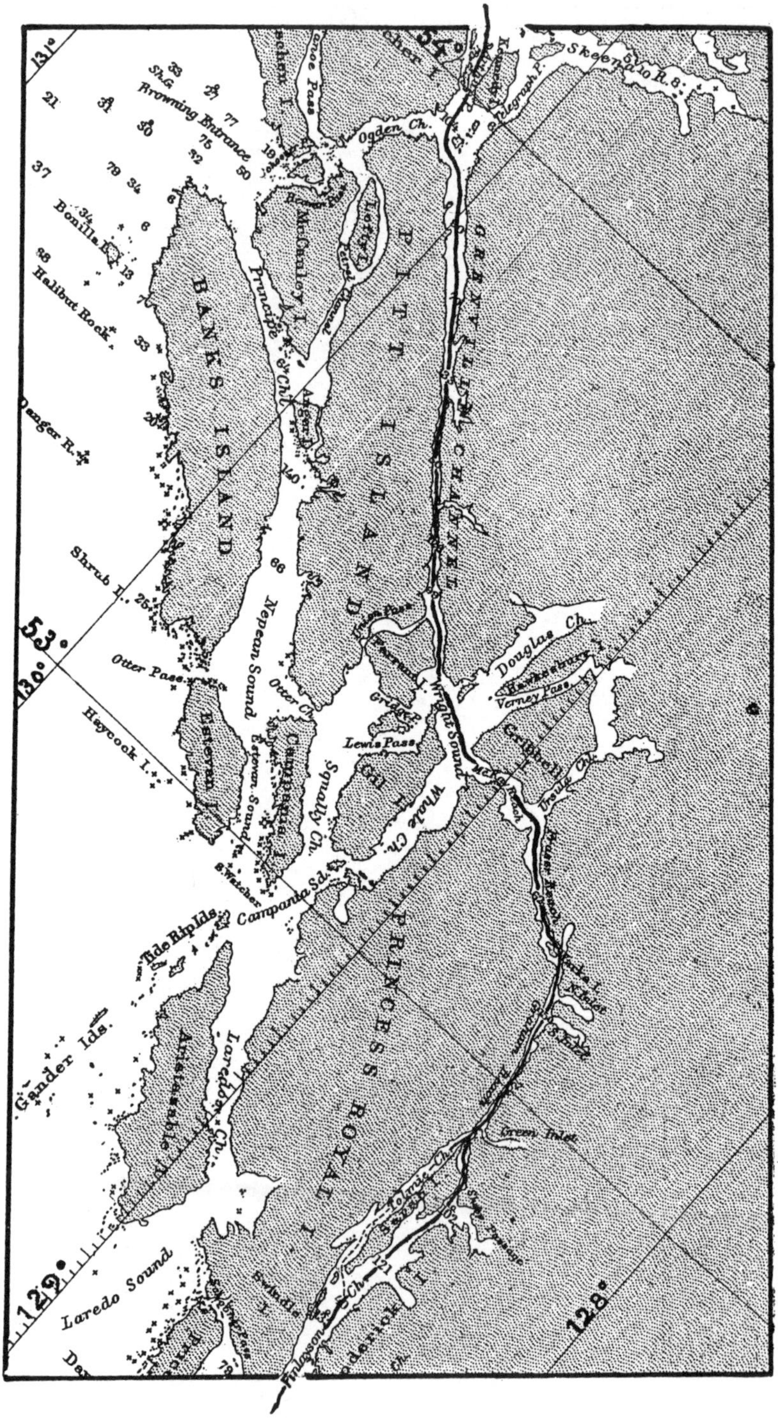

From Finlayson Channel to Malacca Pass.

MAP No. 5.

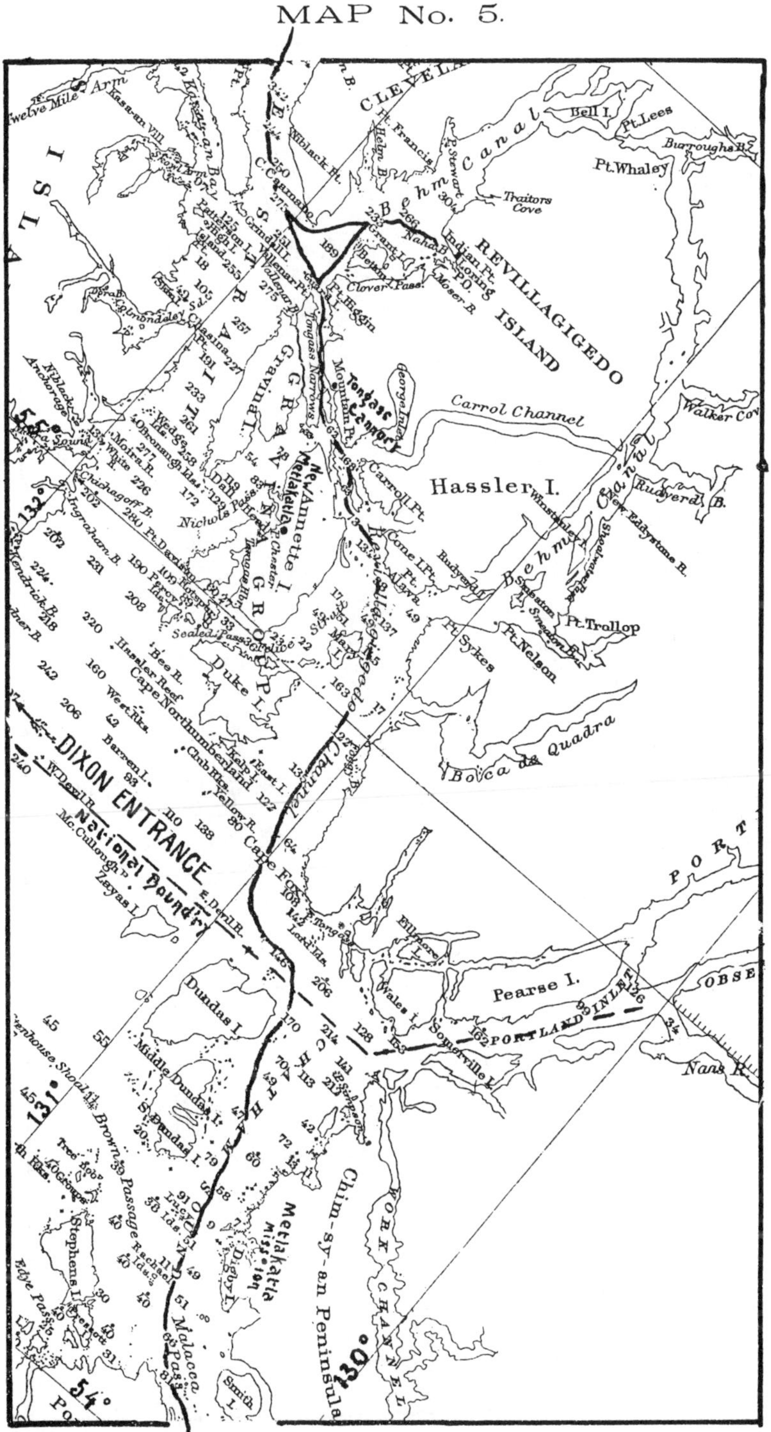

From Malacca Pass to Oleveland Peninsula.

MAP No. 6.

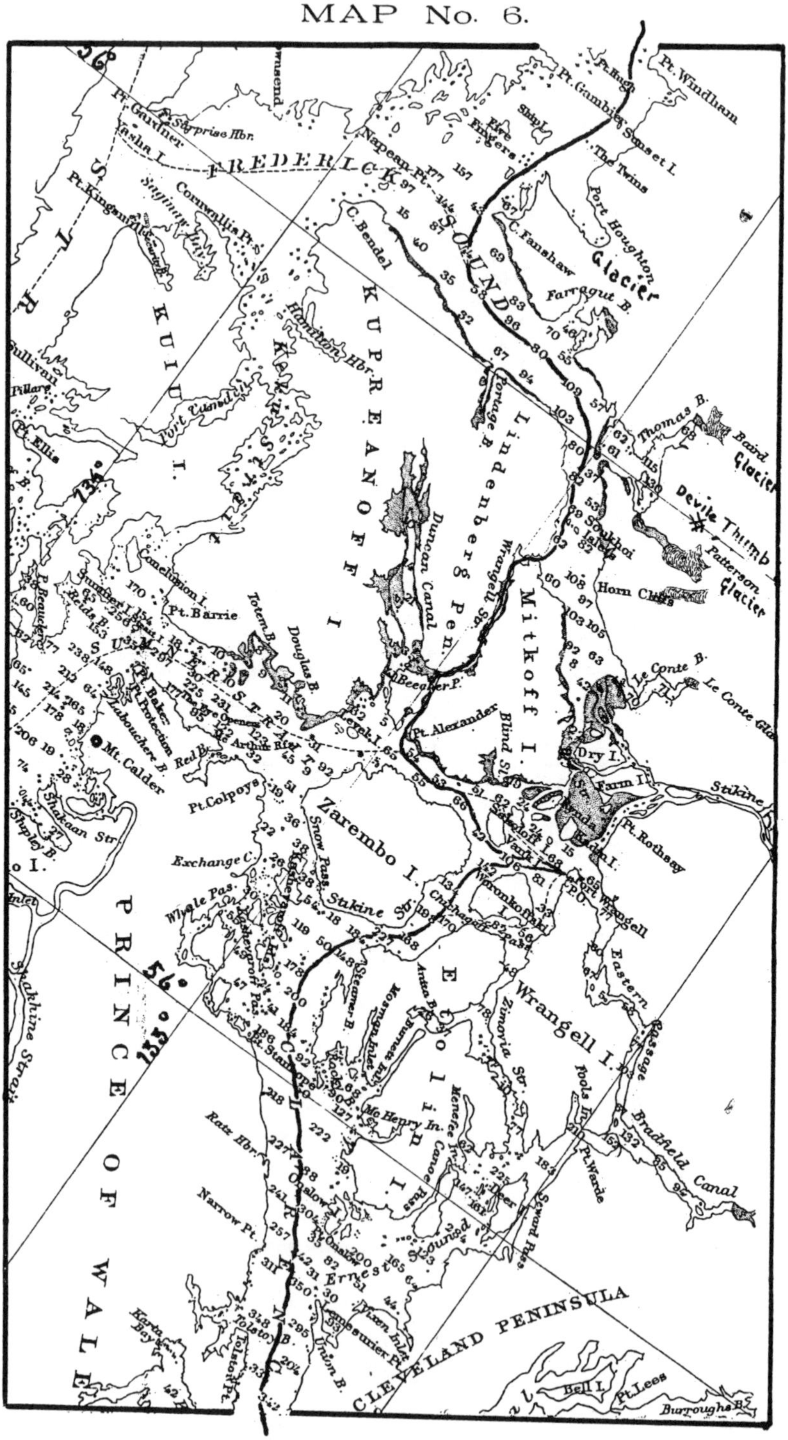

From Cleveland Peninsula to Stephens Pass.

MAP No. 7.

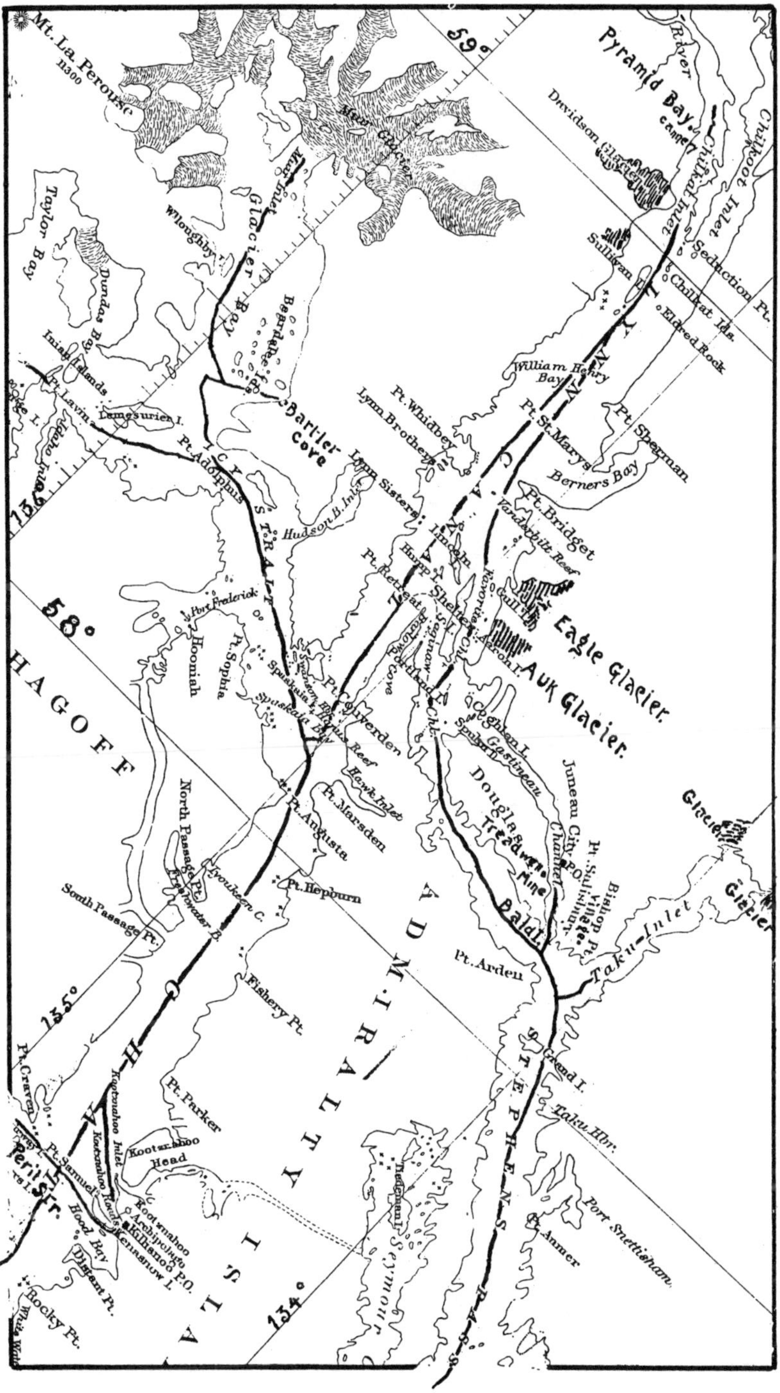

From Stephens Pass to Muir Glacier.

MAP No. 8.

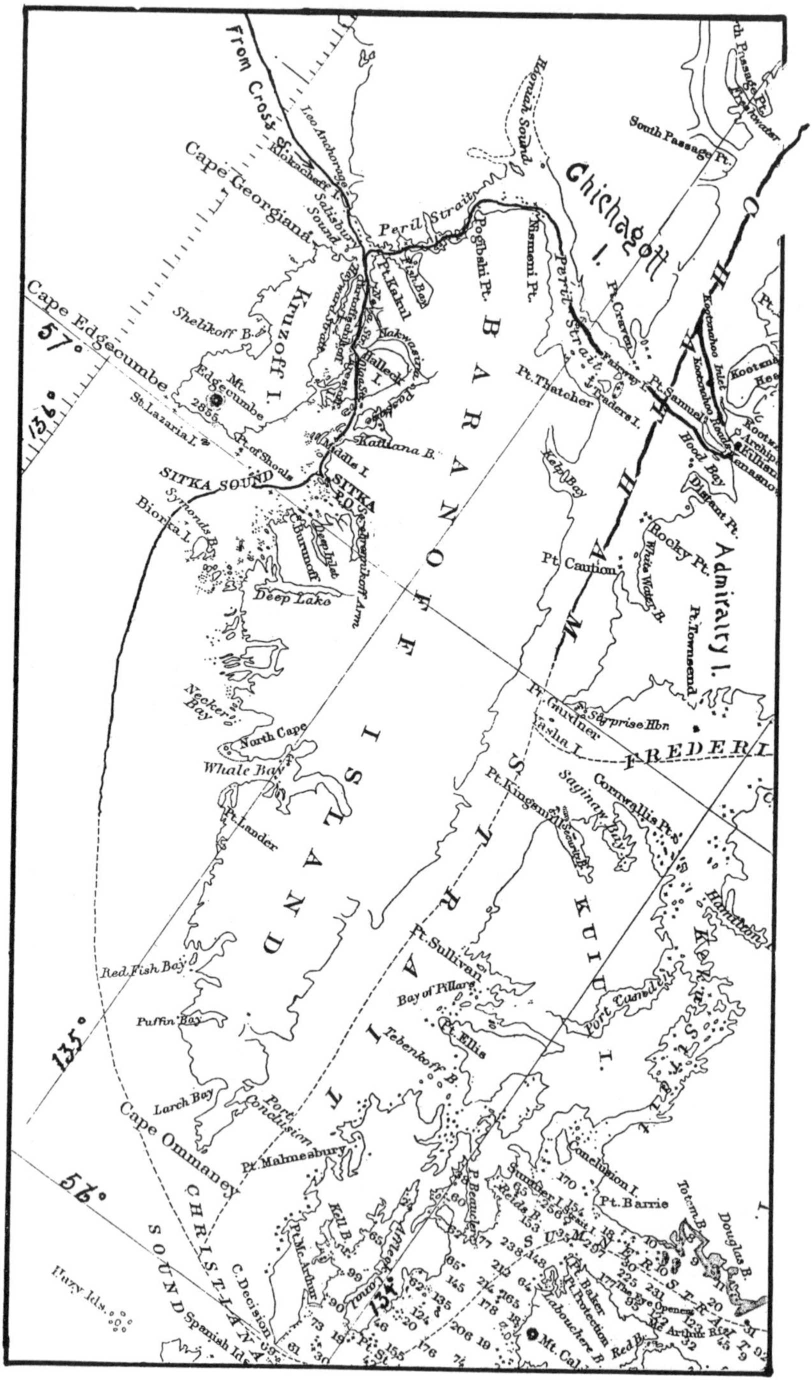

Sitka, Peril Straits and Vicinity.